Sport, Leadership, and Social Inclusion

This book considers how sport organizations can create inclusive practices to strengthen social progress, focusing on the importance of leadership in fostering positive change.

Drawing on original research, and adopting a meso-level, multidisciplinary approach that includes perspectives from sport management, the sociology of sport and organizational psychology, the book considers the evidence for sport as a vector of social progress. Featuring qualitative interviews with non-profit sport leaders from organizations across Europe, the book looks at the conditions under which social inclusion through sport is possible and examines the challenges and opportunities related to three areas of inclusivity and exclusivity: access, participation, and empowerment.

Offering a new perspective on how leadership can help unlock the potential of sport as an inclusive force in society, this book is an important read for anybody with an interest in sport development, sport management, social inclusion, or the relationship between sport and wider society.

Hans Erik Næss is Professor of Sport Management in the Department of Leadership and Organization, School of Communication, Leadership and Marketing at Kristiania University of Applied Sciences, Norway. He has published extensively on sport, governance and management, including The Green Transition in Motorsport: Purpose, Politics, and Profit (Routledge 2024).

Mari Svendsen is Associate Professor of Leadership and Organization in the Department of Leadership and Organization, School of Communication, Leadership and Marketing at Kristiania University of Applied Sciences, Norway. She has published articles on topics such as leadership, social inclusion in sport, voice behaviour, organizational democracy, and meaningful work.

Routledge Focus on Sport, Culture and Society

Routledge Focus on Sport, Culture and Society showcases the latest cutting-edge research in the sociology of sport and exercise. Concise in form (20,000–50,000 words) and published quickly (within three months), the books in this series represents an important channel through which authors can disseminate their research swiftly and make an impact on current debates. We welcome submissions on any topic within the sociocultural study of sport and exercise, including but not limited to subjects such as gender, race, sexuality, disability, politics, the media, social theory, Olympic Studies, and the ethics and philosophy of sport. The series aims to be theoretically-informed, empirically-grounded and international in reach, and will include a diversity of methodological approaches.
Available in this series:

Skateboarding and the Senses
Skills, Surfaces, and Spaces
Sander Hölsgens and Brian Glenney

Essentials of Cerebral Palsy Football
Edited by Iván Peña González, Raúl Reina Vaillo, and Manuel Moya Ramón

National Symbols at the Olympic Games
An Olympics Without Flags?
Jörg Krieger

The Olympic Games, Sports Law and Human Rights
Alexandre Miguel Mestre

Sport, Leadership, and Social Inclusion
Hans Erik Næss and Mari Svendsen

For more information about this series, please visit: https://www.routledge.com/Routledge-Focus-on-Sport-Culture-and-Society/book-series/RFSCS

Sport, Leadership, and Social Inclusion

Hans Erik Næss and Mari Svendsen

LONDON AND NEW YORK

First published 2026
by Routledge
4 Park Square, Milton Park, Abingdon, Oxon OX14 4RN

and by Routledge
605 Third Avenue, New York, NY 10158

Routledge is an imprint of the Taylor & Francis Group, an informa business

© 2026 Hans Erik Næss and Mari Svendsen

The right of Hans Erik Næss and Mari Svendsen to be identified as authors of this work has been asserted in accordance with sections 77 and 78 of the Copyright, Designs and Patents Act 1988.

The Open Access version of this book, available at www.taylorfrancis.com, has been made available under a Creative Commons Attribution-Non Commercial-No Derivatives (CC BY-NC-ND) 4.0 International license.

Any third party material in this book is not included in the OA Creative Commons license, unless indicated otherwise in a credit line to the material. Please direct any permissions enquiries to the original rightsholder.

Trademark notice: Product or corporate names may be trademarks or registered trademarks, and are used only for identification and explanation without intent to infringe.

British Library Cataloguing-in-Publication Data
A catalogue record for this book is available from the British Library

ISBN: 978-1-032-86508-9 (hbk)
ISBN: 978-1-032-86510-2 (pbk)
ISBN: 978-1-003-52784-8 (ebk)

DOI: 10.4324/9781003527848

Typeset in Times New Roman
by SPi Technologies India Pvt Ltd (Straive)

Contents

Acknowledgements   *vi*

1 The role of sport in contemporary society   1

2 Theoretical framework and methodology   16

3 The role of leadership in creating access to social inclusion arenas   34

4 The role of leadership in facilitating participation   55

5 The role of leadership in stimulating empowerment   76

6 The role of leadership for social inclusion policy development in Europe   106

Index   *124*

Acknowledgements

This book is the result of an explorative collaboration process which has afforded us with the greatest of respect for the trailblazers of social inclusion through sport in Europe. Our sincerest thanks go to all of our informants for sharing their time and experiences with us. Without their dedication and hard work, it would not have been so much to write about, even though this book is a drop in the sea compared to what is going on out there. Thanks to the International Sport and Culture Association (ISCA) for input, and thanks to Andrew Milner for his proofreading skills. Many thanks to Simon Whitmore and Rebecca Connor at Routledge for making the road from first contact to published book a smooth ride.

To Jonas, a constant reminder of why inclusion matters. This book is for you and for a world where everyone belongs.

Hans Erik Næss and Mari Svendsen
Kristiania University of Applied Sciences, Oslo, 2025

1 The role of sport in contemporary society

Introduction

In *What is Sport?* originally written in 1960, French philosopher Roland Barthes writes that 'What is it then that men [sic] put into sport? Themselves, their human universe. Sport is made in order to speak the human contract' (Barthes, 2007, p. 65). Be that as it may, neither contracts nor the universality of sport guarantee harmony. Although sport is hailed as an arena where people can realize their need for belonging and where societal value is created, sport is as exclusive as it is inclusive with its regulations, rules, traditions, and norms. Yet, since the 1990s, expectations of sporting organizations to use sport as inclusive arenas and as a contributor to social progress and welfare for all and their ability to do so have become explicit. For example, a report claimed that the annual social value of community sport and physical activity in England was £107.2 billion (Sport England, 2024). In Europe, this expectation is often related to 'the European Model of Sport' (EMS) which has 'produced a multitude of positive benefits, including contributions to education, social inclusion and public health' (EPAS, 2020).

Claims like these rest on a plethora of research which have tried to unravel the role of sport in society and its relationship with social inclusion programmes, initiatives, and actions (Haudenhuyse, 2017; Schaillée et al., 2019). As scholarly interest in sport and social inclusion has grown significantly in the 2010s, a string of new questions and new areas in need of further research have therefore been identified (Waardenburg & Nagel, 2019; Moustakas & Robrade, 2023). Given the reach of organized grassroots sports in Europe, with more than 700,000 clubs and about 60 million members (Seippel et al., 2023, p. 204), contrasted with the fact that only 25% of physically active Europeans participate in organized sports (Rask et al., 2024), there are a number of calls for action for more research on issues related organizational capacities and social inclusion beyond elite sport (Dowling et al., 2021; De Bock et al., 2023). Yet, there is a scarcity of research linking leadership in sports organizations with social inclusion

(Næss & Svendsen, 2025), and in the authoritative report on the future of EMS to the European Commission by Sennett et al. (2022) leadership is mentioned only briefly in relation to gender equality and top-level positions. Therefore, our research question is: *What role does leadership play in promoting social inclusion through sports?*

To answer that, this study cross-pollinates insights from sociology, psychology, leadership, and sport management research, and draws upon a qualitative interview sample of sport leaders (N=37) from 19 European countries. Due to the organizational diversity of European sport, the scope of this book is not limited to certain types of organizations or leadership positions. Instead, its analysis rests on the relationship between leadership and social inclusion activities related to access, participation, and empowerment (Gidley et al., 2010). Our exploration of how these dimensions interlace does not target specific demographics, but concerns a diverse range of groups and individuals vulnerable to social exclusion – people with physical disabilities or mental impairments, immigrants, marginalized youth, or social and ethnic minorities, to name a few. On that basis, the aim of the book is twofold: on the one hand, to provide a new *empirical* perspective on social inclusion in sport through sport leaders, and on the other hand, to provide some *conceptual* clarifications that increase the precision of 'social inclusion' as an analytical term. In what follows, we introduce the backdrop to our study. The chapter ends with some concluding remarks and a reading guide to the rest of the book.

The emergence of sport in society

Sport as an institutionalized dimension of societies is often dated to the 16th century. With the codification and standardization of rules in Great Britain in the 19th century, sport became an international phenomenon (Guttman, 2004). Sport governing bodies in football and athletics were established in the early 1900s to ensure fair play across borders and to increase the popularity of sport. From the beginning, states used sport as a tool to educate the population (in a democratic way) and a means of propaganda (in an authoritarian way). Sport's prominence in world society continued to increase in the 1960s and 1970s when the commercial aspects of events and teams began to take hold. A shift came with the 1984 Olympic Games in Los Angeles as 'the spectacularizing of events' emerged as the norm for the fans' experience of sport. A decade later, this type of sports experience helped transform sport into a lifestyle phenomenon when combined with globalization processes, not least through the information technology and mediatization revolution in the 1990s as well as political exploitation and 'sportswashing' in the 21st century (Beissel & Andrews, 2022).

In the context of these changes, sport came to be increasingly considered part of the European integration project by the European Union (Marivoet, 2014; Porro et al., 2020). From being viewed primarily through an economic lens in the 1970s, a turning point for sport came in 1990 when the Council of Europe (CoE) published the revised version of the European Sport for All Charter. In its original text from 1975, it asserted that: 'Every individual shall have the right to participate in sport' (Council of Europe, 1975). Aware of the role of sport as part of the rejuvenated Europeanization project, political interest in sport was broadened when the European Community became the European Union in 1992, in the form both of major commercial events and of grassroots sports. Despite few changes to the Charter's wording, sport was now explicitly 'an aspect of socio-cultural development related to a wide range of welfare services including education, health, social services, land-use planning and the arts' (Green, 2006, p. 218). A few years later, the 1997 Treaty of Amsterdam recognized the 'the social significance of sport, in particular its role in forging identity and bringing people together' (Treaty of Amsterdam, 1997, p. 136). Shortly after, the Nice Declaration of 2000 underlined how vital sport was 'for integration, involvement in social life, tolerance, acceptance of differences and playing by the rules' (European Council, 2000: Annex IV para 3).

Therefore, Marivoet (2014) argues that since the *White Paper on Sports* by the European Union in 2007, sport has been 'officially' expected to promote social inclusion and public health, the establishment of equal opportunities, and to prevent racism and discrimination at both elite and grassroots levels. His argument is further strengthened by the European Commission's claim in 2011, is that sport 'has a strong potential to contribute to smart, sustainable and inclusive growth and new jobs through its positive effects on social inclusion, education and training, and public health' (European Commission, 2011, p. 2). After the adoption of the UN Sustainable Development Goals in 2015, the European Commission's view was expanded to assert that 'the global phenomenon of sport has the power to connect influential networks of diverse partners and stakeholders with a shared commitment to lasting development' (Lemke, 2016). Finally, the EU's Work Plan for Sport 2024–2027 invites member states to explore sport 'as a framework for personal, social and learning skills and promoting tolerance, solidarity, inclusiveness as well as other sport values and EU values' (Council of the European Union, 2024, p. 6).

As a result, it is no exaggeration to say that the perception of sport's responsibility for societal welfare has grown considerably. Coalter (2015) argues that the early 2000s saw 'a shift from the traditional welfare approach of developing sport in community, to seeking to develop communities through sport (…) as sport promoted itself as being able to contribute to the new, ill-defined "social inclusion" agenda' (p. 20). For example, European governments 'are pressuring federations to contribute more to fulfil their societal role and to cope with the current Sport-for-All trends' (De Bock et al., 2023, p. 1331). Drawing upon a sample of 44,000 respondents in 33 countries, Seippel (2019), p. 327) found that 76% of the respondents *think* that sports 'have a positive integrative effect.' Often, however, the hailing of sport's positive contribution to society lacks political commitment. By comparing how sport clubs in ten European countries promote social inclusion and volunteering, a report from the project 'Social Inclusion and Volunteering in Sports Clubs in Europe' (SIVSCE) from the 2010s states that, in most of the ten countries, 'binding policies and plans are almost absent' (Ibsen et al., 2016, p. 43). Furthermore, the claim that sport may create positive social change is inconclusive.

Scholars have taken various positions along the spectrum of opinion on this claim. Taylor et al. (2015, p. 18) state that there is 'substantial evidence that sports participation improves pro-social behaviour and reduces crime and anti-social behaviour, particularly for young men.' Others, like Verdot and Schut (2012), take an intermediate position by claiming that 'sport can indeed be an effective tool with a certain public, but only when specific material and human conditions are present, and consequently, that its efficiency in this regard is not relevant in most other cases' (p. 203). Ponciano Núñez et al. (2023) underline how higher quality of life among youth was positively correlated with inclusive physical activity but also question how to isolate the contribution of sport. This leads us to the critics, who claim that much research fails to pass what Coalter (2017, p. 19) calls 'the problem of displacement of scope – the process of wrongly generalising micro level (programme) effects to the macro (social).' Focusing on sport's impact on 'social cohesion,' Moustakas and Robrade (2023, p. 1304) argue that 'regarding sport for social cohesion, we neither have a clear definition of what is being achieved nor *how*.'

Despite all these changes and challenges, sport is still seen as a greenhouse for social inclusion and, which is more contested, that the EMS plays a pivotal role for the future of this belief (Sennett et al., 2022). While sporting, national, and regional differences obviously occur in a continent with more than 44 countries, current research and sports organizations (Nagel et al., 2020) underline six characteristics of the model: 1) A pyramidal structure, with sport clubs at its foundation, 2) a solidarity mechanism, ensuring redistribution of funds, 3) reliance on volunteers to run the clubs, 4) activities based on values like inclusion, democracy, and fair play, 5) sporting autonomy, and 6) openness of competitions. The political ambition for keeping this model is clear. In the wake of 'Brexit,' the rise of populism, and 'a disenchanted Europe' in the years prior to COVID-19 pandemic, Porro et al. (2020) observed that European political leaders were in a hurry to express 'their support for a politically ambitious relaunch of the so-called European model' which they saw as 'a project to pursue without further postponements and hesitations' (p. 3). Yet, these characteristics are not merely a top-down product of the EU. A Europe-wide survey from 2021 found that, among 'the majority of respondents,' these six characteristics were 'either very relevant or relevant to the specific sport identified or the organisation of sport in Europe' (Sennett et al., 2022, p. 8).

On the other hand, as the report also highlights, although the model seems relevant to sport organizers, it has been criticized for becoming outdated and not grasping the diversity of European sports activities (Sennett et al., 2022). This has led to bewilderment among stakeholders, Anderson et al. (2023) conclude, more specifically on questions as to how clubs perceive themselves, 'as either passive or active agents within a changing political and societal dynamics' (p. 10). Because of this debate about the role of EMS, 'there is a question of who should be the guardian or provide stewardship to preserve the public interest values and ensure coaches and support staff are equipped to meet all new expectations' (Sennett et al., 2022, p. 9). While this study is not a direct response to this question, it nevertheless uses it as backdrop to advocate a new take on the hitherto rarely explored role of leadership in creating possibilities for social inclusion through sport in Europe. To explain why, we need to address the contentious relationship between sport and social change categorically.

Sport and social change: a contentious relationship

Given the context introduced above it might be said that this book relates to three categories of research linked to sport and social progress. The first category of existing research is 'sport for development' (SFD). As SFD projects are often linked to colonialism and racial hierarchies, reviews show that they take shape as humanitarian initiatives concentrated in Africa and that the most widely used inclusive tool for progress is the game of football (Svensson & Woods, 2017). However, SFD is also criticized for overestimating the importance of sport, claiming that it 'should be viewed and understood (both empirically and strategically) as one element of larger, integrative approaches to development, broadly defined' (Darnell et al., 2022, p. 258).

The second category is about sport and corporate social responsibility. Often drawing on the three-dimensional construct by Carroll (2016) which is relocated from business to sport, it refers to the obligations of businesses to consider the larger, social picture of their activity. Rather than only making a profit for its shareholders or owners, an organization needs to earn legitimacy among its stakeholders and should encompass 'the economic, legal, ethical, and discretionary (philanthropic) expectations that society has of organizations at a given point in time' (Carroll, 2016, p. 2). In the case of sport, this means that organizations have to make explicit a 'concern for social issues and leverage their favored institutional status in helping resolve problems and alleviate human suffering' (Godfrey, 2009, p. 699). Meanwhile, research has identified three critical issues concerning CSR: scope (what is it), accountability (to whom are sports organizations responsible) (Djaballah, 2017), and how is its conceptualization in a sporting context different from or similar to that in the corporate world.

The third category is community development through sports initiatives (Dowling et al., 2021). Empirically, however, sport as a lever for social change through community initiatives has also been criticized for relying on 'fairytale narratives,' deflecting attention from political causes and structural constraints for social progress (Reid, 2017). Conversely, Morgan et al. (2019) examined the potential for sports participation to facilitate the acquisition of positive psychological capital, defined as a composite of self-efficacy, hope, optimism, and resilience. By using data from a British programme called Sporting Youth, aimed at young people aged 13–19 who were considered to be vulnerable and/or at risk, the authors find that 'human and social capital alone cannot deliver social justice and social inclusion to young people residing in disadvantaged localities' (Morgan et al., 2019, p. 1111). And even if they suggest that positive psychological results provide an important piece of 'the social inclusion jigsaw' (p. 1111), the study nevertheless demonstrates the case- and context-based sensitivities involved in social inclusion projects.

As a result, social inclusion is often linked to one or more of these categories, as well as being increasingly promoted as a separate concept for analysis, although the division is not clear-cut. But in contrast to the other three, it has not acquired the same disciplinary identity and continues – despite the increasing political eagerness to use it in policy documents, as shown above – to be a subject of criticism. One of the reasons for this is that social inclusion is conceptualized differently (Cano-Hila, 2022; Pečnikar Oblak et al., 2023) and, most notably in relation to empirical studies, insufficiently attributed to the social inclusion/exclusion matrix in society at large. This was expressed by Anders, a Danish informant from our own interview sample (for more detail, see Chapter 2): 'sometimes it becomes a bit difficult to agree on what we really need to work on together. What do we mean by inclusion in this project? Which partners are involved? What things must we deliver and achieve?' That said, definitions, even though they differ, enable us to discuss their usefulness for academic exploration and identification of new research questions (see also Chapter 6). In the context of EMS, it is noteworthy that a European Council report from 2003 defined social inclusion as:

> ... a process which ensures that those at risk of poverty and social exclusion gain the opportunities and resources necessary to participate fully in economic, social, political and cultural life and to enjoy a standard of living *that is considered normal in the society in which they live*.
>
> (Council of the European Union, 2003, p. 9, italics added)

However, this view ignores the possibility of treating social inclusion and exclusion as separate, but not inseparable, dimensions of social life. It fails to consider the false dichotomy of inclusion and exclusion, which holds that if you are not included, you are excluded (Spaaij et al., 2014).

As important, this relationship between inclusion and exclusion must be interpreted within its own context and with emphasis on certain dimensions of this relationship. Donnelly and Coakley (2002) claimed that researchers were 'deeply suspicious' of sport's potential for promoting social inclusion as they 'have seen little evidence to support the idea that sport is an ideal solution to social *exclusion*, although most could point to some programmes that are organized on a socially *inclusive* basis' (p. 13, italics added). One reason is that sport is neither a mirror of society, nor an economic world of its own with regard to inclusion and exclusion processes (Spaaij et al., 2014; Dugarova, 2015). People have multiple roles and social identities, so that 'they might often simultaneously experience inclusion and exclusion according to specific social power relations' (Elling & Claringbould, 2005, p. 501). As an example, Kelly (2011) found that while social inclusion programmes achieve varying degrees of 'success,' 'their impact on exclusionary processes is inevitably limited' (p. 126).

A way out of this conceptual quagmire is provided by Frisby and Ponic (2013) who on the one hand define social inclusion 'as the process of creating just and equitable *systems* that facilitate people's choices and opportunities to engage (or not) in a wide range of social and democratic activities, including sport and recreation' (p. 381, italics added). On the other hand, they underline that social inclusion, by its very nature, can promote assimilation rather than respecting differences, be assumed to be beneficial when it may not always be, and overlook the fact that 'it is often those who are already included in sport who are deciding how to include those who are not' (Frisby & Ponic, 2013, p. 392). This relational understanding of social inclusion and exclusion in sport, which accounts for the connections between complex and sometimes conflicting forces in play, inspires us to go beyond the system approach by Frisby and Ponic (2013) and explore how leadership agency works in organizations to grasp the various levels of social inclusion and exclusion.

The role of leadership

Leadership in other sectors has been proven to be instrumental in managing social inclusion processes (Leo & Barton, 2006; Kendrick & Sullivan, 2009). That research, however, concentrates on non-sporting fields, so a sport-specific examination of leadership's role in the conditions under which sport can make a difference to social inclusion themes is called for (Swanson & Welty Peachey, 2022). Existing research in sport and social inclusion also focuses on the micro or community level (Schaillée et al., 2019). In line with Suzuki (2017), we, however, argue that the meso level should be explored further because it 'emphasizes the interdependence of individuals in constructing organizational meanings and outcomes' (Bligh et al., 2006, p. 298). According to Gardner and Cogliser (2009) this means:

> the simultaneous examination of at least two levels of analysis where: (a) one or more levels involve individual, dyadic, or group/collective behaviors and processes; (b) one or more levels involve contextual factors, such as organizational of system-wide variables and processes.
> (p. 497)

While we will theorize leadership further and specify the operationalization of this approach in chapters to come, our point of departure is that leadership can be seen as a craft and context-sensitive practice which is relational and interactional, that is, 'more than the work of individuals and their ability to assert influence or power over others. Rather, it is something created through the actions, conversations, language, and interactions between groups of people and within a particular context' (Ferkins et al., 2018, p. 80). However, apart from our own explorations (Næss & Svendsen, 2024, 2025), much of the literature underlines what sport leaders should do rather than what they are doing when managing the issue of combining the exclusionary nature of sport (competition, us vs. them) with its inclusive values (sport is for all, fair play). Moreover, sport in the context of CSR, for example, often treats the organization itself as the decision-making entity, with issues of leadership missing (Sparvero & Chalip, 2022).

On that basis, we contend that although our data set consists of individual leaders, we see them as meso-level 'translators of organizational-level priorities and values so they can be interpreted on the ground in practical terms' (Prime et al., 2021, p. 424) and 'a key source of social information that can significantly influence the formation of a climate for inclusion' (Boekhorst, 2015, p. 242). More specifically, according to Suzuki, there are four lines of action characteristic of leaders' relations-building role in a social inclusion context (Suzuki, 2017). First, she underlines the opportunity for face-to-face human interaction. Drawing upon Sen's capability approach (Sen, 1993), this means addressing how social relations 'are constitutively important if being excluded from them is seen as a loss on its own, whereas they are instrumentally important if exclusion from them results in deprivation in other aspects of life, if not in itself damaging' (Suzuki, 2017, p. 152). Second, there is an opportunity for leaders to enable others to be associated with a social group. Experiencing a sense of belonging can strengthen one's identity and crystallize the meaning of being part of a collective. This perspective:

> ... emphasizes a focus on an individual's interests, strengths and abilities rather than on deficiencies. It also suggests the right of persons to craft and own their unique identity and that others view them as they wish to be viewed or as they view themselves.
> (Scorgie & Forlin, 2019, p. 5)

Third, there is the importance of being part of a formal organizational structure, as underlined by Frisby and Ponic (2013). This means adhering to a set of values and practices that combine rights with duties and opportunities, for example, to have a say in how things ought to be done. Fourth, exploring the three offers above may generate a position in a broader social network. Engaging with a club, for example, brings the possibility of generating social capital which can be converted into other – non-sporting – forms of mastery and self-efficacy (Suzuki, 2017, p. 152), that is, the belief in one's capacity to complete a task, rather than merely possessing the relevant skills.

In practice, as we will document in the upcoming chapters, these four lines of action intersect. The main reason is the extended responsibilities of sport leaders in the 21st century (Næss & Svendsen, 2025). Having to fight within the sporting world for resources, attention, and people, while balancing the playful elements of sport with competing in 'winner-take-all' circumstances, these organizations have moved beyond the realm of governing sporting rules and regulations. Public health, environmental sustainability, digitalization, and social inclusion are but some of the new areas added to strategy prioritizations within sport organizations. At the same time, outside the realm of sport, the competition for welfare means, political distrust in governments, and economic fluctuations challenge the idealized image of sport as driver of 'Social Europe' (Eick et al., 2024). Against this backdrop, we treat social inclusion as part of the leader's challenge to determine what this context means in terms of social complexity with regards to three analytical categories: access, participation, and empowerment (Gidley et al., 2010). This framework was chosen because it offers an opportunity to theorize about, and analyse empirically, how leaders influence the interrelation between what we consider key categories of social inclusion through sport and how it affects people vulnerable to social exclusion.

Concluding remarks

This chapter has introduced our way of exploring the topic of social inclusion through sport. Rather than using related concepts like 'social cohesion' or locating the study within disciplinary boxes like 'sport for development,' we argue that social inclusion as we understand it enables us to explore how leadership can be a pivotal factor in identifying the necessary conditions for making a difference through sport. Unlike the definitions from the CoE and the like above, which include too many dimensions of injustice or inequality to be explorable through our data, this book takes a narrower approach. Our applied definition of social inclusion, based on what we have discussed in this chapter and what is to come in the following chapters, is therefore:

> A process influenced by political, cultural, and economic factors, in which an entity, often a sports organization, seeks to provide access, encourage participation, and enhance empowerment within a community for specific groups, irrespective of their backgrounds. At the same time, it takes into account the risks of assimilation, exclusionary practices, and social pressures that may arise within the community or the inclusion initiative itself.

On that basis, in Chapter 2 we establish a theoretical and empirical baseline for how we explore 'social inclusion.' In Chapters 3–5, this baseline is coupled with a phenomenologically inspired analysis of informants' views on issues of access ('seeing who's not in the room,' see Chapter 3) in relation with participation ('gathering around the table,' see Chapter 4), and the processes of empowerment (utilizing the experience after 'leaving the table,' see Chapter 5). The order of analytical terms and size of chapters are both a result of, and a choice to thoroughly illustrate, the growing intricacy of answering the research question. Lastly, in Chapter 6, we use the interconnections between conceptual and empirical elements to discuss policy implications about leadership and social inclusion through sport and the role of EMS. At the end of each chapter, we present, in table form, the practical implications of the issues raised which take a realistic view of ways in which sport can contribute to social progress.

References

Anderson, K., Book, K., & Norberg, J. (2023). *Challenges and change readiness in grassroot sport*. CHANGE/ENGSO. https://www.engso-education.eu/wp-content/uploads/2023/11/Research-final-w_-cover.pdf

Barthes, R. (2007). *What is sport?* Yale University Press.

Beissel, A., & Andrews, D. L. (2022). Sport, globalization, and glocalization. In L. A. Wenner (ed.), *The Oxford handbook of sport and society*. https://doi.org/10.1093/oxfordhb/9780197519011.013.11.

Bligh, M. C., Pearce, C. L., & Kohles, J. C. (2006). The importance of self- and shared leadership in team based knowledge work: A meso-level model of leadership dynamics. *Journal of Managerial Psychology*, *21*(4), 296–318. https://doi.org/10.1108/02683940610663105

Boekhorst, J. A. (2015). The role of authentic leadership in fostering workplace inclusion: A social information processing perspective. *Human Resource Management*, *54*(2), 241–264. https://doi.org/10.1002/hrm.21669

Cano-Hila, A. (2022). Understanding social inclusion in contemporary society: Challenges, reflections, limitations, and proposals. *Social Inclusion*, *10*(2), 1–5. https://doi.org/10.17645/si.v10i2.5090

Carroll, A. B. (2016). Carroll's pyramid of CSR: Taking another look. *International Journal of Corporate Social Responsibility*, *1*(3). https://doi.org/10.1186/s40991-016-0004-6

Coalter, F. (2015). Sport-for-change: Some thoughts from a sceptic. *Social Inclusion*, *3*(3), 19–23, https://doi.org/10.17645/si.v3i3.222

Coalter, F. (2017). Sport and social inclusion: Evidence-based policy and practice. *Social Inclusion*, *5*(2), 141–149, https://doi.org/10.17645/si.v5i2.852

Council of Europe (1975). *European sport for all charter*. https://www.europa.clio-online.de/Portals/_Europa/documents/B2016/Q_Scholl_Charter.pdf

Council of the European Union (2003). *Joint report by the Commission and the Council on Social Inclusion. Council of the European Union*. http://ec.europa.eu/employment_social/soc-prot/soc-incl/final_joint_inclusion_report_2003_en.pdf. Accessed 12 July 2017.

Council of the European Union (2024). *Resolution of the Council and of the Representatives of the Governments of the Member States meeting within the Council on the European Union Work Plan for Sport (1 July 2024–31 December 2027)*. https://data.consilium.europa.eu/doc/document/ST-9771-2024-INIT/en/pdf

Darnell, S. C., Whitley, M. A., Camiré, M., Massey, W. V., Blom, L. C., Chawansky, M., Forde, S., & Hayden, L. (2022). Systematic reviews of sport for development literature: Managerial and policy implications. *Journal of Global Sport Management*, *7*(2), 249–266, https://doi.org/10.1080/24704067.2019.1671776

De Bock, T., Scheerder, J., Theeboom, M., De Clerck, T., Constandt B., & Willem, A. (2023). Sport-for-all policies in sport federations: An institutional theory perspective. *European Sport Management Quarterly*, *23*(5), 1328–1350. https://doi.org/10.1080/16184742.2021.2009897

Djaballah, M. (2017). *Corporate social responsibility in sport*. In U. Wagner, R. K. Storm, & K. Nielsen (eds.), *When sport meets business: Capabilities, challenges, critiques*. SAGE Publications Ltd. https://doi.org/10.4135/9781473984226

Donnelly, P., & Coakley, J. (2002). *The role of recreation in promoting social inclusion*. Laidlaw Foundation.

Dowling, M., Mackintosh, C., Lee, S., & Allen, J. (2021). Community sport development: managing change and measuring impact. *Managing Sport and Leisure*, *26*(1–2), 1–6. https://doi.org/10.1080/23750472.2020.1854265

Dugarova, E. (2015). *Social inclusion, poverty eradication and the 2030 agenda for sustainable development. UNRISD Working Paper, No. 2015-15, United Nations Research Institute for Social Development (UNRISD)*, Geneva. https://www.econstor.eu/bitstream/10419/148736/1/861278364.pdf

Eick, G. M., Im, Z. J., & Leschke, J. (2024). Towards social Europe? Obstacles and opportunities in the multi-level governance of welfare states. *Social Policy & Administration*, *58*(4), 545–553. https://doi.org/10.1111/spol.13046

Elling, A., & Claringbould, I. (2005). Mechanisms of inclusion and exclusion in the Dutch sports landscape: Who can and wants to belong? *Sociology of Sport Journal*, *22*(4), 498–515, https://doi.org/10.1123/ssj.22.4.498

EPAS (2020). *Position paper on Further Developing the European Sports Model agreed by members of the EPAS Consultative Committee*. https://rm.coe.int/further-developing-the-european-sports-model-european-sportcharter-pa/1680a1b1cf

European Commission (2011). *Communication from the Commission to the European Parliament, The Council, The European Economic and Social Committee and the Committee of the Regions, Developing the European Dimension in Sport*. https://eur-lex.europa.eu/legal-content/EN/TXT/PDF/?uri=CELEX:52011DC0012

European Council (2000). *Conclusions of the Presidency*, Nice 7–10 December 2000. https://www.europarl.europa.eu/summits/nice1_en.htm

European Union (1997). *Council of the European Union, Treaty of Amsterdam Amending the Treaty on European Union, The Treaties Establishing the European Communities and Related Acts*, 10 November 1997. https://www.europarl.europa.eu/topics/treaty/pdf/amst-en.pdf

Ferkins, L., Skinner, J., & Swanson, S. (2018). Sport leadership: A new generation of thinking. *Journal of Sport Management*, *32*(2), 77–81. https://doi.org/10.1123/jsm.2018-0054

Frisby, W., & Ponic, P. (2013). Sport and social inclusion. In L. Thibault, & J. Harvey (eds.), *Sport policy in Canada* (pp. 381–403). University of Ottawa Press.

Gardner, W., & Cogliser, C. (2009). Meso-modeling of leadership: Following James G. (Jerry) Hunt's lead in integrating micro- and macro-perspectives of leadership. *The Leadership Quarterly*, *20*(4), 493–500. https://doi.org/10.1016/j.leaqua.2009.04.001

Gidley, J., Hampson, G., Wheeler, L., & Bereded-Samuel, E. (2010). Social inclusion: Context, theory and practice. *The Australasian Journal of University-Community Engagement*, *5*(1), 6–36.

Godfrey, P. C. (2009). Corporate social responsibility in sport: An overview and key issues, *Journal of Sport Management*, *23*, 698–716. https://doi.org/10.1123/jsm.23.6.698

Green, M. (2006). From 'sport for all' to not about 'sport' at all?: Interrogating sport policy interventions in the United Kingdom. *European Sport Management Quarterly*, *6*(3), 217–238, https://doi.org/10.1080/16184740601094936

Guttman, A. (2004). *Sports: The first five millennia*. University of Massachusetts Press

Haudenhuyse, R. (2017). Introduction to the issue "sport for social inclusion: Questioning policy, practice and research". *Social Inclusion*, *5*(2), 85–90. https://doi.org/10.17645/si.v5i2.1068

Ibsen, B., Nichols, G., & Elmose-Østerlund, K. (2016). *Sports club policies in Europe. A comparison of the public policy context and historical origins of sports clubs across ten European countries*. University of Southern Denmark. https://boris.unibe.ch/96268/1/Ibsen-Nichols-Elmose-Osterlund_Sports%20club%20policies%20in%20Europe.pdf

Kelly, L. (2011). 'Social inclusion' through sports-based interventions? *Critical Social Policy*, *31*(1), 126–150. https://doi.org/10.1177/0261018310385442

Kendrick, M. J. & Sullivan, L. (2009). Appraising the leadership challenges of social inclusion. *The International Journal of Leadership in Public Service*, *5*(2 Supplement), 67–75.

Lemke, W. (2016). The role of sport in achieving the sustainable development goals. *UN.org*, August (no 2), https://www.un.org/en/chronicle/article/role-sport-achieving-sustainable-development-goals

Leo, E., & Barton, L. (2006). Inclusion, diversity and leadership: Perspectives, possibilities and contradictions. *Educational Management Administration & Leadership*, *34*(2), 167–180. https://doi.org/10.1177/1741143206062489

Marivoet, S. (2014). Challenge of sport towards social inclusion and awareness-raising against any discrimination. *Physical Culture and Sport Studies and Research*, *63*(1), 3–11. https://doi.org/10.2478/pcssr-2014-0017

Morgan, H., Parker, A., & Roberts, W. (2019). Community sport programmes and social inclusion: What role for positive psychological capital? *Sport in Society*, *22*(6), 1100–1114, https://doi.org/10.1080/17430437.2019.1565397

Moustakas, L., & Robrade, D. (2023). Sport for social cohesion: From scoping review to new research directions. *Sport in Society*, *26*(8), 1301–1318, https://doi.org/10.1080/17430437.2022.2130049

Næss, H. E., & Svendsen, M. (2024). "We are not selling soap here, you know": Eight humanistic leadership qualities in sport. *Leadership*, *20*(3), 144–161. https://doi.org/10.1177/17427150241237925

Næss, H. E., & Svendsen, M. (2025). Leadership, sport and social inclusion: 'Everything is solvable'. In D. Pearson, K. Hallmann, & J. J. Zhang (eds.), *Diversity, equality, and inclusivity in the global sport community*. Routledge.

Nagel, S., Elmose-Østerlund, K., Ibsen, B., & Scheerder, J. (2020). *Functions of sport clubs in European societies: A cross-national comparative study*. Springer International.

Pečnikar Oblak, V., Campos, M. J., Lemos, S., & Rocha, M. et al. (2023). Narrowing the definition of social inclusion in sport for people with disabilities through a scoping review. *Healthcare*, *11*(16), 2292. https://doi.org/10.3390/healthcare11162292

Ponciano Núñez, P. D., Portela-Pino, I., & Martínez-Patiño, M. J. (2023). Understanding the characteristics of community youth sports programs interventions: A systematic review and recommendations. *Sage Open*, *13*(2). https://doi.org/10.1177/21582440231179206

Porro, N. R., Martelli, S., & Testa, A. (2020). Introduction: Sport and the citizens of a disenchanted Europe. In N. R. Porro, S. Martelli, & A. Testa (eds.), *Sport, welfare and social policy in the European Union* (pp. 3–20). Routledge.

Prime, J., Ferdman, B. M., & Riggio, R. E. (2021). Inclusive leadership: Insights and implications. In B. M. Ferdman, J. Prime, & R. E. Riggio (eds.), *Inclusive leadership. Transforming diverse lives, workplaces, and societies* (pp. 421–429). Routledge.

Rask, S., Le Coq, C., & Storm, R. K. (2024). *European sport: One or several sporting realities?* Play the Game. https://www.playthegame.org/media/0nwbrzf3/european-sport.pdf

Reid, G. (2017). A fairytale narrative for community sport? Exploring the politics of sport social enterprise. *International Journal of Sport Policy and Politics*, *9*(4), 597–611. https://doi.org/10.1080/19406940.2017.1349827

Schaillée, H., Haudenhuyse, R., & Bradt, L. (2019). Community sport and social inclusion: International perspectives. *Sport in Society*, *22*(6), 885–896, https://doi.org/10.1080/17430437.2019.1565380

Scorgie, K., & Forlin, C. (2019). Social inclusion and belonging: Affirming validation, agency and voice. In K. Scorgie, & C. Forlin (eds.), *Promoting social inclusion: Co-creating environments that foster equity and belonging* (pp. 3–16). Emerald.

Seippel, Ø. (2019). Do sports matter to people? A cross-national multilevel study. *Sport in Society*, *22*(3), 327–341. https://doi.org/10.1080/17430437.2018.1490263

Seippel, Ø., Breuer, C., Elmose-Østerlund, K., Feiler, S., Perényi, S., Piątkowska, M., & Scheerder, J. (2023). In troubled water? European sports clubs: Their problems, capacities and opportunities. *Journal of Global Sport Management*, *8*(1), 203–225, https://doi.org/10.1080/24704067.2020.1806493

Sen, A. (1993). Capability and well-being. In M. Nussbaum, & A. Sen (eds.), *The quality of life* (pp. 30–53). Oxford.

Sennett, J., Le Gall, A., Kelly, G., Cottrill, R., Goffredo, S., & Spyridopoulous, K. (2022). *Study on the European Sport model. A report to the European Commission*. https://www.sportesalute.eu/images/studi-e-dati-dello-sport/schede/2022/90-study-europeansportmodel.pdf

Spaaij, R., Magee, J., & Jeanes, R. (2014). *Sport and social exclusion in global society*. Routledge.

Sparvero, E. S., & Chalip, L. (2022). Sport, leadership, and social responsibility. In L. A. Wenner (ed.), *The Oxford handbook of sport and society* (pp. 296–315). Oxford University Press.

Sport England (2024). *The social value of sport and physical activity in England*. https://sportengland-production-files.s3.eu-west-2.amazonaws.com/s3fs-public/2024-10/The%20social%20value%20of%20sport%20and%20physical%20activity%20in%20England%202.03.pdf?VersionId=jvPWYkNVjc0NSfBA8Cx1Vjpa5SAFcSxV

Suzuki, N. (2017). A capability approach to understanding sport for social inclusion: Agency, structure and organisations. *Social Inclusion*, 5(2), 150–158, https://doi.org/10.17645/si.v5i2.905

Svensson, P. G., & Woods, H. A. (2017). A systematic overview of sport for development and peace organisations. *Journal of Sport for Development*, 5(9), 36–48.

Swanson, S., & Welty Peachey, J. (2022). An agenda for future leadership research in sport management: Explorations, considerations, and challenges. In D. Shilbury (ed.), *A research agenda for sport management* (pp. 95–112). Edward Elgar Publishing.

Taylor, P., Davies, L., Wells, P., Gilbertson, J., & Tayleur, W. (2015). *A review of the social impacts of culture and sport*. The Culture and Sport Evidence (CASE) programme. https://assets.publishing.service.gov.uk/government/uploads/system/uploads/attachment_data/file/416279/A_review_of_the_Social_Impacts_of_Culture_and_Sport.pdf

Verdot, C., & Schut, P-O. (2012). Sport and social inclusion: The political position vs. practices. *European Journal for Sport and Society*, 9(3), 203–227. https://doi.org/10.1080/16138171.2012.11687897

Waardenburg, M., & Nagel, S. (2019). Social roles of sport organisations: Developments, contexts and challenges. *European Journal for Sport and Society*, 16(2), 83–87. https://doi.org/10.1080/16138171.2019.1622203

2 Theoretical framework and methodology

Introduction

Social inclusion is a much-used term which must be clarified to improve its analytical precision and practical use for sports organizations. It is therefore imperative to review the conceptual content of social inclusion in relation to 'how society works' to be able to answer questions like 'inclusion of whom, inclusion of what, inclusion into what, how, for what purpose and on what terms' (Dugarova, 2015, p. 2). In order to theorize about conditions under which social inclusion through sport is possible, it is necessary to empirically explore the factors that prevent, and the factors that enable, sports leaders to realize socially inclusive practices. To reduce the number of possible entries to 'social inclusion' and simultaneously make it relevant for leadership and grassroots sports organizations, we advance in this chapter an idea of social inclusion interlinked with managing social complexity.

This idea draws upon Maxwell's (2013) definition of a theoretical *framework*, which includes 'the systems of concepts, assumptions, expectations, beliefs, and theories that supports and informs your research' (p. 39). Applying this framework 'assists the researcher in refining goals, developing research questions, discerning methodological choices, identifying potential threats to validity, and demonstrating the relevance of the research' (Collins & Stockton, 2018, p. 4). Consequently, by drawing upon an abductive methodology and the interview data set described at the end of this chapter, we discuss how leadership for social inclusion through sport is shaped by the way in which societies work and the human interaction they entail. Our use of 'theoretical framework' within the context of sport and social inclusion, enables us in Chapters 3–5 to go deeper into 'theory' in a stricter sense, that is, how the findings connect to a coherent explanation about 'social life that holds transferable applications to other settings, context, populations, and possibly time periods' (Saldaña & Omasta, 2018, p. 257; cited in Collins & Stockton, 2018, p. 4).

DOI: 10.4324/9781003527848-2

This chapter has been made available under a CC-BY-NC-ND license.

With these choices in mind, we turn in the next section to a discussion of how inclusion and exclusion are part of any society. Besides providing the necessary context to theorize further social inclusion challenges in sport, the aim of this chapter is to justify the use of the three dimensions of social inclusion in Chapters 3–5 instead of just one. Lastly, the chapter combines theories of social transactions, complexity leadership theory (CLT), and inclusive leadership theory in a sports context. Since the mid-2000s, CLT has gained a foothold in organizational studies, as it 'proposes that adaptability, which enhances performance and innovation, occurs in the everyday interactions of individuals acting in response to pressures and opportunities in their local contexts' (Arena & Uhl-Bien, 2016, p. 23). As it is less explored in a sports context, this chapter takes the opportunity to advocate its relevance and address its flaws to serve as an exploratory concept useful to empirical studies of social inclusion in sport.

The integration of society

Sport has long been hailed as a neutral resort for dialogue and development of the best in humankind. Nelson Mandela, former president of South Africa and one of the architects of the removal of the racist apartheid regime, said at the inaugural Laureus World Sports Awards in 2000 'sport has the power to change the world' and his words have subsequently been taken as a truth for what sport can be (Mandela, 2000). A similar sentiment was shared by Eleni, a Cypriot informant from our sample (see end of this chapter):

> Working towards social inclusion helps drive positive change and it's beautiful to see diversity in sport. The work is definitely rewarding and also appreciated by the people who you are giving a chance to be seen, who might else not get that chance. It's about being human.

Notwithstanding Mandela's and Eleni's sincere belief and laudable work to make this happen, sport is no unicorn for peaceful progress. Seippel's list (2019) of sport's unattractive qualities includes 'doping, cheating, injuries, violence, corruption, hooliganism, fanaticism, nationalism, eating disorders, male chauvinism, narrow-mindedness, smugness, commercialization and too much (or too little) elite sports at the expense of grassroots sports' (p. 328). To understand the importance of this observation, and to specify the role of leaders in these conflicting circumstances, we need to explore how societies 'work' in relation to inclusion and exclusion dynamics (Allman, 2013; see also Chapter 6).

Societies are possible for a variety of reasons. According to historical accounts of their development, albeit not always in agreement (Elias,

1991; Graeber & Wengrow, 2023), the easiest way to that development is that all societies possess different integration systems and mechanisms for creating a compromise between the individual and the collective. Humans have managed to develop institutions, norms, and cultures which ensure that there is some level of stability in economic and political organization and adherence to common values. These characteristics are formed by our relationship with geography, climate, and resource base. However, because people and ecologies are different across the globe, societies have organized themselves differently both geographically and throughout history. This affects their view of inclusive and exclusive practices and their ideological and political rationale. One reason is that 'what we call society is merely one set of human interrelations among several of varying scale and comprehensiveness into which people are classifiable or classify themselves, often simultaneously and with overlaps' (Hobsbawm, 1971, p. 30).

To unpack the contemporary relation between individuals, groups, and societies, which effectively impacts the level of inclusiveness and exclusionary practices on any level of sport, 'complex relationality' is a keyword (Urry, 2005). In a globalizing world, 'small changes make for big differences and lots of things are out to play, together' (Byrne, 2007, p. 18). But in contrast to chaos, Byrne (2007) continues, there is some coordination behind the complexity around us though this does not provide a constant state of equilibrium. Although the past is always with us, contemporary circumstances both shape the limits and opportunities of societal change today as well as in the future, which constantly evolves as a set of shifting relationships and interdependencies (Barth, 2007). Considering the diversity of inclusion and exclusion mechanisms around the world, Allman (2013, p. 7) argues that such 'society-specific particulars might take the form of traditional and historic patterns of stratification, or be based on how individual groups and/or characteristics may be valued over others.'

To understand these particulars, Eriksen (2007) argues that a key question is: *What are the criteria of exclusion and inclusion in a given social environment?* (p. 1060, italics original). Although the international codification of sport is often dated to the 16th century (see Chapter 1), sport is more than rules and regulations. Rather, as argued by Collins (2013), modern sport emerged because of its relationship with the development of a capitalist society in Europe in the 18th century and the concurrent ideological parallels between competition and social order. The reason why sport was codified in the UK, therefore, was not so much to do with the innovative brilliance of English sports administrators as with the reluctance among pre-capitalist aristocrats in mainland Europe to get rid of conventional views of physical competition. A couple of centuries later, this relationship between sport and society has been cemented as a core feature of societies across the world because 'modern sport owes its growth to its symbiotic relationship with the media industry of print, radio and television, the development of a national economy and nationalism, and the creation of a mass, urbanised working class' (Collins, 2013, p. 126).

Coming nearer to our own time, research demonstrates how sports organizations integrate market-driven, values-driven, and policy-driven logics in a unique way, and therefore operate with sectoral overlap that creates a grey area between business, civil society, and politics (Misener & Misener, 2017; Gammelsaeter & Anagnostopoulos, 2022). We therefore need to identify the elements of social organization in the modern world. Bernard, one of our French informants, said that approaching social inclusion issues in sport required much more from leaders than they were aware of:

> Let's first look at society as a whole, like, let's zoom out. We've got so many crises. The way we solve them usually is by using band-aid… how do you actually zoom *in* and go to the root causes of where the problem comes from, and then kind of rechange and reinvent the system? It's not about tweaking. It is really like, 'do you reinvent it or do you rebuild this from scratch kind of thing' with all your experience? That's social inclusion.

Elaborating on this point, it can be argued that a key component of understanding social complexity is how actors desire to optimize their own life chances, either on behalf of themselves or on behalf of their group. In a leadership context, Podolny et al. (2006) put it well: 'It is the role of leadership to turn an organization into an institution, by infusing the organization with values and creating a distinct organizational identity and sense of purpose that is in fact internalized by organizational members as meaningful' (p. 8). But leaders are dependent on others to make this happen. Against this backdrop, we might see models of social organization as derived from an anthropological view of transactions, that is, 'the process which results where the parties in the course of their interactions systematically try to assure that the value gained for them is greater or equal to the value lost' (Barth, 1966, p. 4; see also Barth 1972, 2007).

Barth adds that while this does not cover all human interaction or social relations, as people interact for other reasons and motives than to seek maximum gain, in the situations where 'people shape their decisions and actions in a relationship by a transactional accounting, systematic and cumulative effects ensue that will determine many features of that relationship' (Barth, 2007, p. 8). Moreover, decisions are usually made between alternatives. The preferability of the alternatives, in turn, is 'influenced by certain constraints and incentives' (Barth, 1966, p. i); these comprise the parametric conditions of the choice situation (Skvoretz & Conviser, 1974, p. 54). Which alternative is preferred and, eventually, which decisions are actually made, depends on whether the individual or individuals making the decision, i.e., the leader or leaders – orient themselves towards self-gain or value which is optimal for the sum of the partners (Barth, 1966, p. 4; Skvoretz & Conviser, 1974, p. 54). For example, our informant Aila, from Finland, who had been working with social inclusion in club and federation settings, said that

> if you do inclusive actions, you can make more people feel welcome and welcome new people. But it doesn't necessarily mean that if you don't do these inclusive actions, you are excluding. It can happen that someone gradually starts to feel excluded.

In other words, paraphrasing Barth's theory, we can view transactions, which are based on a given set of alternatives, as a way to exploit social relations leaders are involved in for the benefit of the stakeholders.

While this model of social organization characterizes many types of interaction in society, it could be argued that in the sporting sector where the European Model of Sport (EMS) is considered, a unique challenge emerges as the complexities of leadership in non-profit sports 'are rarely seen in other forms of governance in the forprofit and nonsporting domains' (O'Boyle et al., 2019, p. 189). Above all, drawing on the theoretical framework of institutional logics, a study reports that many national federations 'experience multi-level complexity when responding to numerous, often conflicting, requirements coming from: commercial, government, and social logics' (Pedras et al., 2020, p. 483). To illustrate our approach to these challenges, the following section discusses the relationship between inclusion/exclusion in how it affects the way we view societal complexity and the role of leaders.

The relationship between social inclusion and exclusion

In many ways, society's complexities are sport's complexities, since 'sport does not exist in a societal void and is, as such, often implicated in mechanisms of exclusion in society' (Haudenhuyse, 2017, p. 86). Normative ideals on inclusive practices, ranking the different inclusion dimensions, and considerations of the places people live (Silver, 2015), all affect the relationship with social exclusion. Therefore, it is necessary for sport leaders to be aware of the societal forces involved, even those affecting the game negatively. A study of fears of Islamic radicalization through sports in France identified social exclusion based on a schismogenetic (i.e., type of arm's race) logic: When players with North African origins joined a football club, or when those already there became victims of political fear, societal prejudice pervaded the clubs. But instead of football becoming middle ground for diplomacy, this external influence reinforced a group identity 'on both sides' that had been less pronounced before (Sallé & Bréhon, 2020). These variations and many more, necessitate addressing the normative foundation for what counts as inclusion in sport specifically, especially when factoring in societal structures and transactional mechanisms discussed above.

Our French informant, Sabine, with experience of a variety of capacity-building projects among youth, said that the barriers to inclusion came from forces in society:

> If we look beyond sports, I think it all goes back to dominant culture or norms. And this dominant group is – I'm saying this also without judgment, I'm not accusing – being reluctant or unable to change somehow and to open up.

A practical example was given by a Slovenian informant, Judit, who recalled having meetings with parents in the club about including youth with disabilities in ordinary sporting activities: 'We were talking about this openly. And I had about maybe five people that actually ended to come to our club because they were not feeling well being around people with disability.' Relatedly, Labonte (2004) asks: 'how does one go about including individuals and groups in a set of structured social relationships responsible for excluding them in the first place?' (p. 117). On the one hand, it is easy to be sympathetic to this perspective because of the material and class-based components of sport, which Labonte (2004) emphasizes as key to social exclusion in general. Similarly, United Nations Department of Economic and Social Affairs (UNDESA) (2010) argue that 'social inclusion processes require both addressing the drivers of exclusion, including certain policies and institutions as well as discriminatory attitudes and behaviours, and actively "bringing people in"' (p. 22). As an example, from sport, Elling and Claringbould (2005) claim that:

> Socialization, money and time, accessibility of sporting facilities, normative and discriminating structures and cultures, and sporting abilities and talent are interacting in/exclusionary factors that influence sport participation options among people with different social-status positions (e.g., age, gender, and ethnicity).
>
> (p. 498)

On the other hand, as addressed in Chapter 1, it is not certain that instances of social exclusion and inclusion are correlational or can be explained by the same reasons. Above, we cited informants exemplifying one aspect of it. Another is the role of sport more generally. While the proportion of Europeans who never exercise or play sports was 39% in 2009, it had increased to 46% in 2017 (Rask et al., 2024, p. 8). Within Europe, these numbers vary dramatically, from 78% in Portugal to 8% in Finland (Rask et al., 2024, p. 9). The main reason for this, according to a Eurobarometer survey (2022), is the lack of time (by 41% of respondents), not discrimination, finances, or similar. The second most cited reason was a lack of motivation or interest (25%). Related to the latter, it is noteworthy that 'most EU citizens engage in sport, exercise, or physical activity in informal settings such as parks and outdoors (47%), as part of active transportation (24%), or at home (37%)' (Rask et al., 2024, p. 12). Examining the relationship between physical activity and ethnic minority groups, a Danish study found that the dominating policy focus on sport clubs is not necessarily the most relevant arena for social inclusion as commercial centres and fitness activities are far more popular (Schmidt et al., 2025).

In other words, organized sport cannot be seen as a universal key to social inclusion. It is crucial for leaders to grasp this in order to imagine how social inclusion through sport is possible through different organizational arrangements. To give an example, Aila said that clubs are really into improving their good governance standards. When it comes to social inclusion, however:

> We are really struggling with getting people to see that the social inclusion is really the core thing. And, you know, I have been working with equality questions a long time and social inclusion. And what I have got many times from white privileged men in the 50s, they are saying to me like social inclusion is not the core of sports.

By contrast, Sennett et al. (2022) conclude in their review of the European Model of Sport's status that many stakeholders think that the model:

> ...ought to have a more explicit focus on particular European values that should be promoted (for example, democracy, labour rights and human rights). This is an important finding in terms of raising expectations towards the sport federations on their civic responsibility.
> (Sennett et al., 2022, p. 84)

Conversely, for leaders to grasp this interrelation of inclusion/exclusion levels in the context of sport's role in society more generally, the question of what sport is for needs to be answered. One line of research addresses the possible turn from the 'winning at all costs' ideology that has characterized many sports in the past decades, at least in the Anglo-Saxon world, to 'success beyond winning' (Burton & Leberman, 2017), as well as differences between individual lifestyle sports (like snowboarding) and traditional team sports (like football). Rindler et al. (2022) suggest that the performance focus in organized sports 'can be a reason for dropouts among a significant number of adolescents, and these reasons are more predominant among adolescent girls' (p. 863), whereas unorganized sport offers more autonomy and fewer hierarchies. Yet few dropout studies mention social inclusion in any committing way. Even when it is part of the picture, it might be given a low priority compared with responses to other things sport is supposed to engage in. Sabine, a French informant, told us that it is hard to be very positive about inclusion when you struggle to find money for basketballs, before underlining: 'Those struggles are real.' To explore what it would take for leaders to close the gap between policy wishes and everyday practices, in addition to the mulitiplicity of considerations in terms of the most appropriate organizational form, we now turn to leadership theory.

Elements of sports leadership in a complex world

For leaders to grasp the inclusion-exclusion dynamic in society, it is necessary to expand the basic idea of leadership introduced in Chapter 1. Former theorizations on how sports leaders lead in this respect is traditionally characterized by borrowing concepts and ideas from other spheres of society. From the mid-1990s to the present, however, 'sport management leadership researchers began to investigate tasks and skills associated with leadership in the sport context' (Welty Peachey et al., 2015, p. 573), yet with transformational leadership as a key principle in much of it. Welty Peachey et al. (2015) exemplify this by outlining how transformational leadership and gender issues were coupled to analyse the status of organizational performance. Meanwhile, Welty Peachey et al. (2015) also argue that there 'is a critical need to incorporate multilevel investigations into our work to develop sport-focused leadership theory and the boundary conditions under which such theory will operate' (p. 578).

Whereas this call has been met by innovative explorations of sports leadership connected to gender equality (Sotiriadou & de Haan, 2019), diversity and inclusion (Cunningham, 2019), and elite sport (Andersen et al., 2022), scholarly developments have also been constrained by how 'leadership research in sport management has been dominated by leader-centric notions' and by the way that most researchers 'take an abiding essentialist perspective toward leadership' (Billsberry et al., 2018, pp. 171–172). Furthermore, scholars have argued that sport leadership in general has yet to acknowledge the ramifications of a patriarchal culture and structures which work against gender equity, unintentionally upheld by researchers who fail to acknowledge the inherent bias in the imported concepts (Leberman & Burton, 2017). At the same time, research has uncovered many opportunities that are unused with regard to forging new connections between societal sectors and organizational levels when it comes to developing leadership in sport. Merging the findings from our earlier studies (Næss & Lange, 2022; Næss & Hanssen, 2023; Næss & Svendsen, 2024, 2025) generates a picture of sport leaders struggling to cope with organizational ambidexterity, structural constraints, and the maintenance of personal purpose.

Taking this into account, we argue that a relevant stepping stone is CLT. Here, leadership is understood as a set of interactions between different people in various roles and capabilities 'from which a collective impetus for action and change emerges' (Uhl-Bien et al., 2007, p. 299). Because these interactions move between systems, organizations, and sectors, this interplay is managed by three types of activities by leaders (Uhl-Bien et al., 2007). The first type is adaptive leadership. Instead of being 'an act of authority,' adaptive leadership refers to adjustments of what Lichtenstein et al. (2006) call complex adaptive systems (CAS). Relationships in these systems are not primarily defined hierarchically, as they are in bureaucratic systems, but by interactions between those involved. This activity is thus characterized by somebody managing its facilitative potential for change (Lichtenstein et al., 2006; Uhl-Bien et al., 2007). The second type is administrative leadership. This refers to those in formal managerial roles who coordinate actions. The third type is enabling leadership, which works as a balancing mechanism for the previous two types by merging the need for stability and innovation (Uhl-Bien et al., 2007). Although basing this conceptual trio on bureaucratic organizations, the theory's key proponents nevertheless suggest that it offers a perspective on 'organizational leadership that recognizes the necessarily intertwined and meso nature of administrative (formal) and adaptive (informal) dynamics in organizations' (Uhl-Bien & Marion, 2009, p. 646).

Notably, the three entangled CLT functions in bureaucratic organizations – administrative leadership, adaptive leadership, and enabling leadership (Uhl-Bien & Marion, 2009, p. 633) – are also often found in sports organizations (Næss & Hanssen, 2023; Næss & Svendsen, 2025). People with experience of positions integrating these functions and their interrelatedness therefore became a criterion for our interview sample. While we concur with the views of leadership as a relational process rather than being placed in the hands of a few selected individuals, roles and positions with formal or informal responsibilities must nonetheless be filled by *someone*. These individuals, either together or on their own, practise inclusive leadership for many reasons and in many ways but are – as we will return to in later chapters – united by a belief in the importance of personifying encouragement for a common cause. As such, they stand on the shoulders of a rich history of leadership, where scholars have, at least since Chester Barnard's *The Function of the Executive* from 1938, been concerned with the human dimensions rather than performance, effectiveness, and resource maximization. According to Barnard, the responsibility of the leader was the 'securing, creating, inspiring of "morale" in the organization' (Barnard, 1938, p. 279). The emphasis on social inclusion as part of this understanding of leadership as something more than realizing the rational aims of an organization is of a much newer date.

The work by Brewer (1991) was instrumental in putting the social into the analysis of an individual's need for belonging and uniqueness, which in a workplace context, became the responsibility of leaders. Expanding this to a stakeholder view, leadership behaviours associated with exclusion and inclusion can, however, emerge from different motives (Shore & Chung, 2023). For example, exclusion of one or more individuals might be necessary to secure inclusion of the majority. By contrast, inclusion can be motivated by a desire to expand the in-group either by changing the norms of belongingness or the values of uniqueness. Moreover, leaders must balance neutrality and positive discrimination to grasp diversities in needs and wants among stakeholders (Nishii & Leroy, 2022). In some cases, 'a person's need for acceptance can be *oppositional* to that person's active need to be valued as unique from others' (Thompson & Matkin, 2020, p. 19, italics added). Lastly, there are some paradoxes of inclusion that cannot be solved, only lived with. For example, some organizations promote exclusion through a talent management architecture 'that focuses on the identification and development of a few selected employees, while simultaneously, organizations promote inclusion, in the attempt to minimize existing inequalities for traditionally marginalized groups' (Daubner-Siva et al., 2017, p. 315). As both talent management and diversity management is part of modern organizations, they must co-exist in ways that at a certain point will be of disadvantage to one or the other.

Our study of sport and social inclusion, however, offers a way to bridge these concerns, while making it possible to rectify one of the criticisms against CLT, namely 'how leadership emerges and the dynamics of the relational interactions among organizational agents' (Tourish, 2019, p. 223). To flesh out this claim, we combine the theoretical input from Barth, CLT, and inclusive leadership to explore in the next chapters Gidley et al.'s (2010) three dimensions of social inclusion:

> The narrowest interpretation pertains to the neoliberal notion of *social inclusion as access*; a broader interpretation regards the social justice idea of *social inclusion as participation*; whilst the widest interpretation involves the human potential lens of *social inclusion as empowerment*.
> (Gidley et al. 2010, p. 2)

Based on interview data presented below, we will explore how leadership is related to these dimensions before suggesting in Chapter 6 how they are interrelated in this study as baseline for new perspectives on social inclusion through sport. The reason for dividing Gidley et al.'s categories into separate analyses is that, as they co-exist and interweave with the relational complexities of social inclusion and exclusion discussed above, they must be connected to the main tasks leaders perform in their positions: act in accordance with the values of sport, organize for things to happen in an effective way, and facilitate communication between relevant parties. To explain how this is managed in grassroots sport across Europe, we now turn to data and methods.

Data and methods

Much of the theoretical framework for this book, introduced above, was settled before the authors set out to gather data. As a result, this study is based on an abductive research design, where 'theoretical understanding sets parameters to what they [the researchers] are initially looking for' (Thompson, 2022, p. 1411). Central to this approach is a sample of 37 informants aged 25–62 (19 male and 18 female) from 19 European countries. Recruitment was based on a key informant view, that is, strategically engaging people whose:

> areas of expertise are usually limited to specific areas pertaining to their professional or activist roles in a community, roles that shape their understanding and interpretation of circumstances, behaviors, and motivations for these behaviors.
> (McKenna & Main, 2013, p. 117)

Criteria for identifying these roles were that informants had experience of positions where administrative, adaptive, and enabling leadership functions (Uhl-Bien & Marion, 2009; see also Chapter 2) were combined or intertwined. At the same time, we corroborated the insights of the informants by triangulating interview data with secondary data from project websites, research literature, and policy programme reports and surveys by civil society organizations and the European Commission. As a consequence, the book explores leadership 'using a first-person "as-lived" phenomenological inquiry' (Souba, 2014, p. 78), which entails qualitative interviews with sport leaders about their experience of the research topics. Given the differences of accessibility and interviewee preferences, the interviews were a mix of in-depth semi-structured interviews and online qualitative survey interviews (Kvale, 1983; Braun et al., 2021). Findings from these interviews, as well as from secondary data were analysed by following the process of phenomenological inquiry (Hycner, 1985; Groenewald, 2004).

The first step of this process is called bracketing and phenomenological reduction. According to Hycner (1985), it involves 'using the matrices of that person's world-view in order to understand the meaning of what that person is saying, rather than what the researcher expects that person to say' (p. 281). The second step is to explicate the data into 'units of meaning' (Groenewald, 2004, p. 50). Sometimes referred to as coding, this means highlighting words and extracts from interviews. Because most informants were non-native English speakers, citations are sometimes grammatically adjusted to clarify the meaning. The third step is to cluster these units of meaning into themes. Due to our use of access, participation, or empowerment as key categories of social inclusion, the themes we generated from the explication step, were placed in the category which made most sense when it came to understanding the phenomenon of social inclusion through sport. The fourth step, which concerns empirical validation of the data's relevance to the phenomenon as a whole (the holistic motive) and justification for this placement (the elimination of redundancies), is provided in each of Chapters 3–5. The final step, which is placed in Chapter 6, contains the writing up of 'a composite summary, which must reflect the context or "horizon" from which the themes emerged' (Groenewald, 2004, p. 51).

To ensure the trustworthiness of these findings and the process leading to them, the study utilized Tracy's (2010) checklist for quality in qualitative research. A summary of the process is found in Table 2.1.

Table 2.1 Eight criteria for quality in qualitative research

Criteria for quality	Indicators	Keys to this study
Worthiness of topic	Timeliness, considering societal developments	The study responds to calls for research on how sport can be socially inclusive
Rich rigor	Appropriate choice and use of theory and data	The study draws on a qualitative sample of leaders to fill a gap in the literature and to address hitherto less explored theoretical perspectives
Sincerity	Transparency about the methods and challenges	The analytic procedure of the study is made explicit in a coherent way
Credibility	Thick description, concrete detail, explication of tacit (non-textual) knowledge, and showing rather than telling	The study contains many citations from the sampled leaders to illustrate the research topic and expose what may be taken for granted
Resonance	Evocative representation of findings	The study is written in a book format that encourages the authors to be sharp and direct in their narrative style

(*Continued*)

Table 2.1 (Continued)

Criteria for quality	Indicators	Keys to this study
Significant contribution	Proving its value to the academic and sporting community	The study's worth has been confirmed by the interview sample (so-called 'member checks') by sharing some findings while writing has progressed
Ethical	Compliance with ethical standards for research	The study is approved by the Norwegian ethical committee for research (SIKT)
Meaningful coherence	A logical connection between literature, research questions/foci, findings, and interpretations	The study's use of a conceptual framework to structure the contents is equivalent to the 'breadcrumb trail' of the exploration

Source: Adapted from Tracy (2010, p. 840).

To demonstrate our application of these criteria, the remaining chapters of this book are written with the intention of conveying its analytical solidity. Our blend of theory and data, choice of narrative style, selection of explanatory words as well as quotations and stories from our informants, and text structure within and between chapters, are means to support our methodological approach as well as to underpin the iterative exploration of, and phenomenological approach to, the research question.

Concluding remarks

This chapter has outlined a theoretical framework in line with Maxwell's (2013) definition of how we must integrate ideas on social inclusion into the matrix of society. The rationale for acknowledging this view is that sport does not exist in isolation from other spheres in society. Leaders in these spheres and sectors, moreover, are bound to different social systems, organizations, and relations, and to different conceptualizations and levels of social inclusion, which all affect their ability and desire to make decisions on behalf of their sport and their stakeholders. Paraphrasing Elias (1991), this means that sport leaders must consider how societies work only insofar as they manage the balance between the needs of individuals with the demands of the collective through a social order.

Theorizing on how social organization emerges through a certain type of transaction between its members or stakeholders for a sporting organization, enabled us to combine basic premises for human interaction with CLT and relate it to sport leadership. In practice, this means that leaders are facing the challenge of advocating social inclusion projects through sport by specifying their relevance – especially on behalf of an organizational unit, such as a club, association, or a federation – to society in general. Given the complexity of the relationship between sport and society, and the diverse aims sport organizations are intended to serve on behalf of various stakeholders on different levels (from the global to the individual), leadership becomes central to *convincing* others about the value of inclusivity through sport in the first place, *facilitating* the implementation of projects, and making sure of *connecting* the aim to a relevant outcome.

If sport is to provide ideas and practices to an inclusive society, or even function as a conflict-reducing mechanism, its exclusionary connotations and practices related to this social order and the conditions it brings for social inclusion must also be addressed (cf. Sallé & Bréhon, 2020). In the next chapters, consequently, we will draw upon our empirical sample of sport leaders in Europe to analyse how they view social inclusion opportunities and barriers related to access, participation, or empowerment. While there are other ways of conceptualizing sport and social inclusion, and the framework itself is rudimentary for our purposes, these three dimensions encapsulate an exploratory merger of our activity-based approach (see Chapter 1) and leadership theorizations (this chapter). This people-centred view not only enables us to examine the role of sport in a social inclusion context, but, as we will return to in Chapter 6, also generates insights into how to address opportunities and limits to sport's inclusive potential in the future.

References

Allman, D. (2013). The sociology of social inclusion. *SAGE Open*, *3*(1). https://doi.org/10.1177/2158244012471957

Andersen, S. S., Hansen, P. Ø., & Houlihan, B. (eds.). (2022). *Embedded multi-level leadership in elite sport*. Routledge.

Arena, M., & Uhl-Bien, M. (2016). Complexity leadership theory: Shifting from human capital to social capital. *People & Strategy: Journal of the Human Resource Planning Society*, *39*(2), 22–27. http://www.sageways consulting.com/wp-content/uploads/2017/03/ComplexityLeadership Theory_HRPS_39.2_Arena_Uhl_Bien.pdf

Barnard, C. (1938). *The functions of the executive*. Cambridge University Press.

Barth, F. (1966). *Models of social organization*. Royal Anthropological Institute, Occasional Paper 23. Glasgow University Press.

Barth, F. (1972). Analytical dimensions in the comparison of social organizations. *American Anthropologist*, *74*(1/2), 207–220. https://doi.org/10.1525/aa.1972.74.1-2.02a01720

Barth, F. (2007). Overview: Sixty years in anthropology. *Annual Review of Anthropology*, *36*, 1–16. https://doi.org/10.1146/annurev.anthro.36.081406.094407

Billsberry, J., Mueller, J., Skinner, J., Swanson, S., Corbett, B., & Ferkins, L. (2018). Reimagining leadership in sport management: Lessons from the social construction of leadership. *Journal of Sport Management*, *32*(2), 170–182. https://doi.org/10.1123/jsm.2017-0210

Braun, V., Clarke, V., Boulton, E., Davey, L., & McEvoy, C. (2021). The online survey as a qualitative research tool. *International Journal of Social Research Methodology*, *24*(6), 641–654. https://doi.org/10.1080/13645579.2020.1805550

Brewer, M. B. (1991). The social self: On being the same and different at the same time. *Personality and Social Psychology Bulletin*, *17*, 475–482.

Burton, L. J., & Leberman, S. (2017). New leadership: Rethinking successful leadership of sport organizations. In L. J. Burton, & S. Leberman (eds.), *Women in sport leadership* (pp. 148–161). Routledge.

Byrne, D. (2007). *Complexity theory and the social sciences*. Routledge.

Collins, C. S., & Stockton, C. M. (2018). The central role of theory in qualitative research. *International Journal of Qualitative Methods*, *17*(1). https://doi.org/10.1177/1609406918797475

Collins, T. (2013). *Sport in capitalist society. A short history*. Routledge.

Cunningham, G. B. (2019). *Diversity and inclusion in sport organizations: A multilevel perspective*. (4th ed). Routledge.

Daubner-Siva, D., Vinkenburg, C. J., & Jansen, P. G. W. (2017). Dovetailing talent management and diversity management: The exclusion-inclusion paradox. *Journal of Organizational Effectiveness: People and Performance*, *4*(4), 315–331. https://doi.org/10.1108/JOEPP-02-2017-0019

Dugarova, E. (2015): *Social inclusion, poverty eradication and the 2030 agenda for sustainable development. UNRISD Working Paper, No. 2015-15*, United Nations Research Institute for Social Development (UNRISD), Geneva. https://www.econstor.eu/bitstream/10419/148736/1/861278364.pdf

Elias, N. (1991). *The society of individuals*. Bloomsbury (org. 1939).

Elling, A., & Claringbould, I. (2005). Mechanisms of inclusion and exclusion in the Dutch sports landscape: Who can and wants to belong? *Sociology of Sport Journal*, *22*(4), 498–515. https://doi.org/10.1123/ssj.22.4.498

Eriksen, T. H. (2007). Complexity in social and cultural integration: Some analytical dimensions. *Ethnic and Racial Studies*, *30*(6), 1055–1069, https://doi.org/10.1080/01419870701599481

Eurobarometer (2022). *Sport and physical activity*. Special Eurobarometer 525. https://europa.eu/eurobarometer/api/deliverable/download/file?deliverableId=83654

Gammelsaeter, H., & Anagnostopoulos, C. (2022). Sport management: Mission and meaning for a new era. *European Sport Management Quarterly*, *22*(5), 637–642. https://doi.org/10.1080/16184742.2022.2100918

Gidley, J., Hampson, G., Wheeler, L., & Bereded-Samuel, E. (2010). Social inclusion: Context, theory and practice. *The Australasian Journal of University-Community Engagement*, *5*(1), 6–36.

Graeber, D., & Wengrow, D. (2023). *The dawn of everything. A new history of humanity*. Picador Paper.

Groenewald, T. (2004). A phenomenological research design illustrated. *International Journal of Qualitative Methods*, 3(1), 42–55. https://doi.org/10.1177/160940690400300104

Haudenhuyse, R. (2017). Introduction to the issue "sport for social inclusion: Questioning policy, practice and research". *Social Inclusion*, 5(2), 85–90. https://doi.org/10.17645/si.v5i2.1068

Hobsbawm, E. J. (1971). From social history to the history of society. *Daedalus*, 100(1), 20–45. http://www.jstor.org/stable/20023989

Hycner, R. H. (1985). Some guidelines for the phenomenological analysis of interview data. *Human Studies*, 8, 279–303. https://doi.org/10.1007/BF00142995

Kvale, S. (1983). The qualitative research interview. *Journal of Phenomenological Psychology*, 14(1–2), 171–196. https://doi.org/10.1163/156916283X00090

Labonte, R. (2004). Social inclusion/exclusion: Dancing the dialectic. *Health Promotion International*, 19(1), 115–121. https://doi.org/10.1093/heapro/dah112

Leberman, S., & Burton, L. J. (2017). Why this book? Framing the conversation about women in sport leadership. In L. J. Burton, & S. Leberman (eds.), *Women in sport leadership* (pp. 1–16). Routledge.

Lichtenstein, B. B., Uhl-Bien, M., Marion, R., Seers, A., Orton, J. D., & Schreiber, C. (2006). Complexity leadership theory: An interactive perspective on leading in complex adaptive systems. *Emergence: Complexity and Organisation*, 8(4), 2–12. https://digitalcommons.unl.edu/managementfacpub/8/

Mandela, N. (2000). Speech at the 20th Anniversary Laureus World Sports Awards. Retrieved from YouTube at https://youtu.be/y1-7w-bJCtY?si=0U7_Hdy0V0330Tis

Maxwell, J. A. (2013). *Qualitative research design: An interactive approach*. SAGE.

McKenna, S. A., & Main, D. S. (2013). The role and influence of key informants in community-engaged research: A critical perspective. *Action Research*, 11(2), 113–124. https://doi.org/10.1177/1476750312473342

Misener, K. E., & Misener, L. (2017). Grey is the new black: Advancing understanding of new organizational forms and blurring sector boundaries in sport management. *Journal of Sport Management*, 31(2), 125–132. https://doi.org/10.1123/jsm.2017-0030

Næss, H. E., & Hanssen, T. A. (2023). 'The only person you can delegate tasks to is yourself'. Leadership challenges and turnover in national federations of sport. *Scandinavian Sport Studies Forum*, 14, 1–27. https://sportstudies.org/2023/03/01/the-only-person-you-can-delegate-tasks-to-is-yourself-leadership-challenges-and-turnover-in-national-federations-of-sport/

Næss, H. E., & Lange, B. K. (2022). Developing organisational ambidexterity in sport organisations? A qualitative study of a mentor programme for young leaders. *European Journal for Sport and Society*. https://doi.org/10.1080/16138171.2022.2075135

Næss, H. E., & Svendsen, M. (2024). "We are not selling soap here, you know": Eight humanistic leadership qualities in sport. *Leadership*, *20*(3), 144–161. https://doi.org/10.1177/17427150241237925

Næss, H. E., & Svendsen, M. (2025). Leadership, sport and social inclusion: 'Everything is solvable'. In D. Pearson, K. Hallmann, & J. J. Zhang (eds.), *Diversity, equality, and inclusivity in the global sport community*. Routledge.

Nishii, L. H., & Leroy, H. (2022). A multi-level framework of inclusive leadership in organizations. *Group & Organization Management*, *47*(4), 683–722. https://doi.org/10.1177/10596011221111505

O'Boyle, I., Shilbury, D., & Ferkins, L. (2019). Toward a working model of leadership in nonprofit sport governance. *Journal of Sport Management*, *33*(3), 189–202. https://doi.org/10.1123/jsm.2018-0227

Pedras, L., Taylor, T., & Frawley, S. (2020). Responses to multi-level institutional complexity in a national sport federation. *Sport Management Review*, *23*(3), 482–497, https://doi.org/10.1016/j.smr.2019.05.001

Podolny, J. M., Khurana, R., & Hill-Popper, M. (2006). Revisiting the meaning of leadership. In B. M. Staw, & R. M. Kramer (eds.), *Research in organizational behavior* (pp. 1–36). Elsevier Science/JAI Press.

Rask, S., Le Coq, C., & Storm, R. K. (2024). *European sport: One or several sporting realities?* Play the Game. https://www.playthegame.org/media/0nwbrzf3/european-sport.pdf

Rindler, V., Luiggi, M., & Griffet, J. (2022). Fostering unorganized sport to sustain adolescent participation: Empirical evidence from two European countries. *Sport, Education and Society*, *27*(7), 862–877. https://doi.org/10.1080/13573322.2021.1923472

Saldaña, J., & Omasta, M. (2018). *Qualitative research: Analyzing life*. SAGE.

Sallé, L., & Bréhon, J. (2020). La radicalisation dans le sport au prisme de la sociologie de Norbert Elias: des commérages aux logiques de l'exclusion. *Staps*, *128*, 61–79. https://doi.org/10.3917/sta.128.0061

Schmidt, E. B., Elmose-Østerlund, K., & Ibsen, B. (2025). A survey study of physical activity participation in different organisational forms among groups of immigrants and descendants in Denmark. *BMC Public Health*, *25*, 345. https://doi.org/10.1186/s12889-025-21314-5

Seippel, Ø. (2019). Do sports matter to people? A cross-national multilevel study. *Sport in Society*, *22*(3), 327–341. https://doi.org/10.1080/17430437.2018.1490263

Sennett, J., Le Gall, A., Kelly, G., Cottrill, R., Goffredo, S., & Spyridopoulous, K. (2022). *Study on the European Sport model. A report to the European Commission*. https://www.sportesalute.eu/images/studie-dati-dello-sport/schede/2022/90-study-europeansportmodel.pdf

Shore, L., & Chung, B. G. (2023). Enhancing leader inclusion while preventing social exclusion in the work group. *Human Resource Management Review*, *33*(1). https://doi.org/10.1016/j.hrmr.2022.100902

Silver, H. (2015). *The contexts of social inclusion.* DESA Working Paper No. 144 ST/ESA/2015/DWP/144. https://www.un.org/sites/un2.un.org/files/2020/08/1597341726.915.pdf

Skvoretz, J. V., & Conviser, R. H. (1974). Interests and alliances: A reformulation of Barth's models of social organization. *Man, 9*(1), 53–67. https://doi.org/10.2307/2800036

Sotiriadou, P., & de Haan, D. (2019). Women and leadership: Advancing gender equity policies in sport leadership through sport governance. *International Journal of Sport Policy and Politics, 11*(3), 365–383. https://doi.org/10.1080/19406940.2019.1577902

Souba, W. W. (2014). The phenomenology of leadership. *Open Journal of Leadership, 3*, 77–105. http://doi.org/10.4236/ojl.2014.34008

Thompson, H., & Matkin, G. (2020). The evolution of inclusive leadership studies: A literature review. *Journal of Leadership Education, 19*(3), 15–30. https://doi.org/10.12806/V19/I3/R2

Thompson, J. (2022). A guide to abductive thematic analysis. *The Qualitative Report, 27*(5), 1410–1421. https://doi.org/10.46743/2160-3715/2022.5340

Tourish, D. (2019). Is complexity leadership theory complex enough? A critical appraisal, some modifications and suggestions for further research. *Organization Studies, 40*(2), 219–238. https://doi.org/10.1177/0170840618789207

Tracy, S. J. (2010). Qualitative quality: Eight "big-tent" criteria for excellent qualitative research. *Qualitative Inquiry, 16*(10), 837–851. https://doi.org/10.1177/1077800410383121

Uhl-Bien, M., & Marion, R. (2009). Complexity leadership in bureaucratic forms of organizing: A meso model. *The Leadership Quarterly, 20*, 631–650. https://doi.org/10.1016/j.leaqua.2009.04.007

Uhl-Bien, M., Marion, R., & McKelvey, B. (2007). Complexity leadership theory: Shifting leadership from the industrial age to the knowledge era. *The Leadership Quarterly, 18*(4), 298–318. https://doi.org/10.1016/j.leaqua.2007.04.002

UNDESA (2010). *Analysing and measuring social inclusion in a global context.* A study prepared by Anthony B. Atkinson and Eric Marlier. UN. https://www.un.org/esa/socdev/publications/measuring-social-inclusion.pdf

Urry, J. (2005). The complexities of the global. *Theory, Culture & Society, 22*(5), 235–254. https://doi.org/10.1177/0263276405057201

Welty Peachey, J., Damon, Z. J., Zhou, Y., & Burton, L. J. (2015). Forty years of leadership research in sport management: A review, synthesis, and conceptual framework. *Journal of Sport Management, 29*(5), 570–587. https://doi.org/10.1123/jsm.2014-0126

3 The role of leadership in creating access to social inclusion arenas

Introduction

The first dimension of the social inclusion model by Gidley et al. (2010) is access. Although this model does not involve sports, it is nevertheless relevant to our study as this dimension entails a neo-liberal perspective where 'access may be regarded as a sufficient expression of social inclusion due to the neoclassical economic conceptualization of human beings as autonomous rational decision makers free from social power imbalances' (p. 3). A little less instrumental, yet not unrelated, perspective is found in sport where 'a good supply of sport infrastructure fosters sport participation' (Hallmann et al., 2012, p. 4). But as we will explore in this chapter, access in a social inclusion debate is more than 24/7 open badminton halls, debates on universal design, or informative websites, as the topic includes political, cultural, and social barriers to inclusion. According to Cass et al. (2005), who analysed the relation between mobility, access, and social circumstances:

> improving access is a complex matter because of the range of human activities that might need to be 'accessed' (...) and that some dimensions of access are only revealed through changes in the infrastructure that 'uncover' previously hidden social exclusions.
>
> (p. 539)

One example is that there are major differences in participation between groups with equal access to facilities (Liu et al., 2008). By problematizing what should be accessed by whom, this chapter explores the context in which barriers to access occur to specify its relevance to lowering the mismatch between needs and offers. Whereas the European Model of Sport (EMS) and studies of it mainly refer to access in terms of overcoming resource shortages (Future ++, 2020; Somerset & Hoare, 2018), we examine how sport leaders may play a role in managing social complexities related to a diversity of accesses as part of social inclusion projects.

DOI: 10.4324/9781003527848-3

This chapter has been made available under a CC-BY-NC-ND license.

To explore an understanding of 'access' as it relates to other dimensions of inclusion, this chapter is structured as follows. The next section sheds light on the complexities of access. Then, we turn to three elements of access which leaders need to consider. Thereafter, we discuss how access to processes where things are decided is as important as physical access to sport facilities. The reason is that, as there are many stakeholders involved, access is granted against various priorities, which necessitates a more holistic approach to this dimension of social inclusion than is often used. The chapter ends with some remarks on how access constitutes the bare necessity of social inclusion thinking which therefore has to be supplemented by research on participation and empowerment.

The complexities of access

A general impression we – the authors of this book – have of social inclusion through sport as it is portrayed in EU policy documents, NGO reports and the like, often starts with an idea of identifying one group in need of being included. Members of this group, thereafter, are recruited by initiative-takers to be part of a sporting activity which allows them to feel part of society in a new way. Besides achieving health benefits and a greater sense of meaningfulness, the sense of achieving group companionship and perhaps insider status in the community makes society work better as sport erases differences and highlights our commonalities. In reality, however, things are a bit more complex, not least because inclusion is seen as something other than integration. Cora, an informant from the Netherlands, said:

> Inclusion in sport goes beyond just being welcomed; it involves being treated fairly and having equal opportunities, both in participating in sports and in coaching/leadership roles. Everyone should be welcome to participate in sport, regardless of gender, background, disability, or religious belief.

These distinctions between inclusion and other concepts highlight a problem with the view of access as a self-explanatory dimension of social inclusion, as if there is nothing left to do once access is provided. For example – and this relates to our discussion of the interrelatedness of social inclusion and exclusion in Chapters 1 and 2 – Waring and Mason (2010) cite an informant who said that: 'You can't just include individuals by not excluding' (p. 522). Relatedly, Karl, one of our informants from Austria, told us a story about a social inclusion project aimed at Afghan female migrants: 'They wanted to learn swimming. And I always thought that [this city], you know, they go out and say they have all the infrastructure. It's very well organized and run, we have the infrastructure, and we have the sport facilities.' Other data confirms this impression. In a report on how cities can contribute to social inclusion through sport (Kunz et al., 2021), in which the anonymized city Karl mentioned took part, it is claimed that sports programmes 'are a cost-efficient means to promote inclusion and social cohesion in the city' (p. 11). To Karl and the Afghan women, however, the city did not assist them much in realizing this principle:

> We were looking for more than nine months for a swimming pool to have these young women, also elder women, to train or to learn swimming. Yes, they had to be behind closed doors, no men around. And we have connections to the city and everything. There are private pools around as well… and we thought this is maybe easier and with some money, but that was also very, very difficult. There are these bureaucratic arguments, you know. Some wanted to help, but they said, we have the sport clubs and they need the lanes. And this is the working hours of our staff and blah, blah, blah. So it's also a bit of a reality check that not everything is so super.

Like many other leaders in sport facing what they see as unfair resistance (Næss & Svendsen, 2024), Karl's voice saddened when he unpacked the chain of barriers to this group. At the same time, the annoyance of having political promises about an inclusive society broken for material, municipal, and cultural reasons, did not seem to affect him beyond a moment's frustration – this was seemingly normal. Being a leader who deals with access-related issues requires patience with how societies work.

One takeaway from the conversation with Karl was that you cannot exploit the role of sport in a social inclusion context unless you consider the multiple levels of inclusion and exclusion in society as a whole. As addressed in Chapter 2, this means accounting for the sometimes ideographic interrelatedness of inclusion and exclusion when assessing the feasibility of social inclusion projects. At the same time, sport is not the same as society but it draws upon certain cultural and social norms to which the understanding of inclusion is adapted. So, what is the alternative to resignation? More money and facilities to all? Not necessarily. While Karl's story illustrates the complexity of this project in particular, it also highlights how access is a multifaceted issue in a social inclusion context. It should be said that no one is expecting leaders to be able to change society towards a more inclusive attitude or build new swimming pools. What they can do, as underlined by many of our informants, is to clarify the interconnections between social inclusion through sport as an aim, a process, and a goal (cf. Dugarova, 2015) and the conditions in which something is doable. Earlier studies have also discovered that Muslim women 'have a difficult time participating in sports due to a lack of women only facilities' (Hallmann et al., 2012, p. 3). According to a Danish informant, Anders, this is not only a democratic incentive, but it is also essential to map the needs 'out there' in society:

> I mean, it would be great if we could filter out what the essentials of what people come and tell us about the world. This is not the case in practice. We're trying to figure out a little bit, 'what's going on? What do our members say? What do we discover? What do we observe? What can we read about'? And then we try to meet these needs. So, it [the organization] is not directly needs-driven, but I think that when we do activities, it is very much about getting the users themselves involved.

Consequently, leaders do have an unused potential in shaping the understanding of access as part of sport's social inclusion aims. At the same time, Gidley et al. (2010, p. 8), who discuss social inclusion with reference to the educational system, exemplify access with topics like equity scholarships, improved infrastructure, and physical access. In sport, other dimensions affect the understanding of access. Discussing the inclusivity factors of physical activity Fehsenfeld (2015; drawing upon Cochrane & Davey, 2008) argues in favour of a shift away from the individual to a more social ecological focus, where 'activities must be arranged in a way that makes them available, accessible, affordable, acceptable, and appropriate to the targeted group' (p. 33). For that reason, 'access' as entry options to sport facilities must be unpacked from its neo-liberal simpleness and repacked as sociological-conceptual construct to suit the complexities of sport before we turn to what leaders can do about it. In what follows, we draw upon a sociological outlook to propose three elements of access which need to be considered.

Physical, political, and socio-cultural barriers

After having identified those in need of socially inclusive activities, the first barrier is to find a location, somewhere to be for a reasonable price. A report from an international consortium of Europe-based organizations working to enhance social inclusion for children through sport underlines that 'practical barriers are grouped into three: time, location, and cost' (Future ++, 2020, p. 20). Similarly, a European Commission report identified external barriers as

> the lack of sport infrastructure, lack of appropriate sport offer, lack of settings favourable to sport practice, high cost of practicing sport, lack of friendly environment for sport practice, or lack of a partner to engage in a sport practice with.
>
> (European Commission, 2021, p. 8)

Obviously, socio-economic issues are present as it costs money to use sport facilities. It can be argued that the higher the socio-economic circumstances, the higher the sport participation (Richard et al., 2023), in addition to the claim that socio-economic status may be advantageous in a socialization context (Pot et al., 2016).

Yet, as evidenced by Karl's story, while the physical facilities and socio-economic circumstances are inescapable parts of the problem, neither explains everything. For example, Florent, one of our informants from France, associated social inclusion through sport with 'no barriers, financial, economical, educational, information… to access at any level, practice, coaching, working, volunteering,' which may impact the level of sport activities in many ways. Analysing youth dropout in sport, which continues the discussion of the multitude of inclusion-exclusion dynamics addressed in Chapter 2, Persson et al. (2020) make a distinction between sport-internal and sport-external reasons. Whereas respondents' views on the former category mentioned practices like too much competitiveness and results orientation, leading to social misery, none in the latter group mentioned lack of facilities. Instead, the sense of belonging – almost regardless of everything else on offer – was found as the most pressing issue (see also Chapter 5). In a broader perspective, as underlined by Cass et al. (2005), it is crucial in debates on access to map 'the time and space patterns of peoples' lives and what these mean for their membership or non-membership of certain social categories' (p. 543). Similarly, the Future ++ report asks: 'what hourly availability does the sports organization offer and how could it fit the needs of children and their families' (Future ++, 2020, p. 43).

For reasons just discussed, we arrive at the second barrier, which is the process leading to physical entry – for example informing the targeted groups about the offer, what it entails, and how suitable access can be discussed. These factors can be as important as the facilities themselves. Whereas leaders are not able to synchronize everybody's lives to ensure access to socially inclusive arenas, they can clarify the necessary conditions for being seen as a legitimate user of for example, sporting facilities. Jakob, an informant from Austria, underlined that leadership could stand in the way of social inclusion 'when performance objectives clash with social objectives.' Relatedly, Kung and Taylor (2014) found that the level of sporting activities for the disabled did not necessarily depend on physical access to the facilities, but on the presence of competent staff at a sport centre. Karl recounted his attempts to find out who to talk to in order to get the Afghan women registered as a group eligible for the use of public facilities. This information is not usually posted on any public website, and furthermore, says Karl:

> The infrastructure is owned to a large degree by the municipality, and they allocate training facilities… have lists and there are clubs who

train. And as a newcomer, it's difficult. A newcomer would have to go to the back of the line and to wait until an opportunity arises.

Local authorities, facility owners, and sport management norms in a given country therefore play a major part in defining access. In Norway, Bergsgaard (2017) has examined how the building, operation, and use of sport facilities is a thoroughly politicized process with municipalities and investors having as much, or more, to say about how facilities should benefit sport rather than its users. Moreover, while the most powerful sport stakeholders end up defining the user profile of, for example, multipurpose halls, Bergsgaard (2017) argues that this reproduction of power structures may not benefit the national aim of physical activity for all, which in a social inclusion context is more relevant than performance-based prioritization of training times and elite recruitment. Hence, the negotiations for access are dependent on where in line the targeted group is found, or placed, by those in power.

This line is affected by the third barrier, which is the intervention of societal discourse in local initiatives and the role of sport in general. On a national or European level, sport, as noted in Chapter 1, is often seen as a central contributor to social cohesion, public health, and intercultural dialogue. This is reflected by funding schemes, where national policies hand over the responsibility for operationalization to the municipalities, although the differences, according to our informants, are vast and often linked to medals in international competitions or the agendas of the current government. Lessard's examination (2017) of a national fund for preventing delinquency through local sport activities in France, found that sport could not be used as an integrative arena unless the societal issues were dealt with (in terms of e.g., radicalization dangers). Similarly, as voiced by Tasha, a French informant:

> People feel excluded, like, it's not for them… These are the resultant of social constructions that are anchored within people, like boxing is not a sport for little girls, and even if things are slowly changing these invisible barriers are still very much present and powerful.

As a result, if society contains a lot of stereotypes about certain groups, the way from idea to practice might be longer than expected. According to Karl, the debacles with the swimming Afghans were not necessarily only about training schedules, as right-wing anti-immigrant sentiments that were noticeable in Austria at the time could have affected the lack of access:

> Maybe it was fear. If we host these Muslim women, maybe we get a bit of a stigma that we are too open. I was not in every telephone conversation, but it [the rejection] was for very, yeah, bureaucratic

reasons. Other clubs, longer established clubs who had privileges or, yes, of course, they also want to train and maybe also a bit of a fear... 'who are they [the Afghan women]? How would we handle it?' So, it's just maybe also something new and maybe in ten years it will be different.

To Karl, and the Afghan women, this sentiment, whose impact on the process is difficult to pinpoint, mirrors other findings from studies on disability and access. Jones (2010) explains that inclusion must locate disability issues outside the individual as 'it is the responsibility of the society (not just the government, but individual citizens such as shopkeepers, bartenders or headmasters) to dismantle or remove barriers' (p. 59). To identify the interrelatedness of these barriers and facilitate solutions to overcome them, leaders thus have a crucial role in making the commitment stick in the organization on the basis of asking new access-related questions. In Chapter 2 we claimed that socially responsible leaders are in charge of promoting the purpose of the organization and of being the change in terms of what they bring to the field of personal and professional identities. Accordingly, By (2021) argues that leaders need to avoid the situation where

> what is important in the long term for organizations and beyond, but which is more complex to measure and inconceivable to deliver on in the short term, becomes less important to decision-makers looking to secure instant or near instant individual rewards.
>
> (p. 6)

To explain how this approach connects with other empirical findings, we now turn to a section on the key factor in which leadership is critical.

The role of leadership: seeing who's not in the room?

So far, we have established that the access dimension of social inclusion relates to multiple aspects of how societies work to produce inclusion and exclusion (see Chapter 2) as a composite of groups, organizations, political structures, cultural norms, and socio-economic circumstances. Those in power coordinating these networks thus have a great responsibility in ensuring representational fairness, at least in regard to the use of public sport facilities. Yet there is one common denominator to avoid patchy solutions to structural challenges. Given our focus on how leaders in sport organizations work to realize social inclusion projects by making transactions in a complex stakeholder network, the discussion above indicates the need for attention to decision-making processes, as they are central to understanding the relationship between organizational aim, structure, and personnel. Nina from Estonia put it well:

Because you are in a privileged situation, you never realize...who is not in the room. So, I think it's keeping this kind of filter of who is not in the room that should be in mind. And then choose what you can do to wiggle some more of your influence into it.

Assuming that representation is a precondition for having a say in decision-making and recalling how the alternatives between decisions are conditioned by relations, as addressed in Chapter 2, we can view decision-making 'as a social process, with the elements of the process presented in terms of events between people, rather than events that occur within a person' (Vroom & Jago, 1974, p. 744). Leading these processes can be done in different ways, Vroom and Jago suggest, from the autocratic approach, where leaders make the decision themselves, to a consultative variant where the role of a leader is 'much like that of a chairman; coordinating the discussion, keeping it focused on the problem, and making sure that critical issues are discussed' (Vroom & Jago, 1974, p. 747). By testing this theory, Vroom and Jago (1974, 1978) found a high degree of correspondence between managerial behaviour and what the model can explain. Sometimes the leader makes the decision, because that's how the organization is rigged, whereas in other cases, the decision is made by a leadership group or even a board. However, the model does not account for the influence of social interaction between decision-holders which is then used to discuss options and make choices (Tjosvold et al., 1986). Instead, Tjosvold et al. (1986) suggest focusing on 'constructive controversy,' that is, when persons bring different and opposing positions, ideas, information, opinions, and perspectives to bear on a problem and attempt to reach a decision' (p. 127). Similar to Barth's (1972) transaction perspective on human collaboration (see Chapter 2), the reason is that, ideally, decision-makers are better placed to 'understand opposing positions and perspectives, open-mindedly consider opposing ideas and information, and to integrate the best to find effective decision' (Tjosvold et al., 1986, p. 127).

Though it rather idealizes the value of debate, the argument for facilitating constructive controversy goes to show why creating access to the decisions is an equally important leadership task as fighting for allocated training slots, reduced public transport expenses, or free footballs. To ensure fair access as part of social inclusion projects through sport, the topics on the table must be debated within this context and led by someone like Vroom and Jago's chairman type. However, due to the often-undefined institutional status of the groups which are to be included and the multilevel responsibilities of sport leaders (Pedras et al., 2020), they must embody a combination of administrative leadership, adaptive leadership, and enabling leadership (Uhl-Bien & Marion, 2009; see Chapter 2). Although leaders for social inclusion projects may negotiate with those in charge of 'regular' sporting activities, as in the case of Karl and the Afghan women above, leaders must advocate the benefit of social inclusion projects as something different from 'ordinary sports' and at the same time unique on behalf of the target group (in this case, Afghan women).

To do so, our informants often pointed to why the bigger picture matters, which so far has included viewpoints on political and socio-cultural barriers in addition to facility use, to ensure that the people most concerned are represented around the table. Alexandra, from Norway, argued that sport had to consider representation in a whole new way: 'We must have greater diversity. That doesn't mean there are too many white straight men. It means that we must have greater diversity when the decision is made.' As an example, she emphasized the potential of professionalizing volunteering in grassroot sport instead of going in the direction of 'cultural schools' [a private-public offer in Norway to youth interested in art, music, and dance]: 'I think it is completely the wrong way to go, precisely because the social inclusion part is not part of the cultural school concept. You may get more top athletes from it, but I don't give a shit about that.'

A keyword in this respect is inclusive leadership, where 'inclusion requires that all individuals feel able to fully and meaningfully contribute to shared goals regardless of group memberships and to do so without assimilating to established norms or relinquishing any part of their identity' (Roberson & Perry, 2022, p. 758). Thus, it is more than addressing diversity, although that is part of the necessary rethink. For example, Bennett and Hannah (2022), who examined leadership and access in a disability context, warn about making this into a question of equality only, as 'rights-based discourse tended to foster employees' equal access to existing, standard structures. Rather than encouraging transformative access, such efforts reinforce existing structures as natural' (p. 343). Buying into this logic results in a view that leaders are inclusive to the extent they enable 'individuals to access information and resources' and focusing on 'the degree to which individuals feel a part of critical organizational processes' (Roberson & Perry, 2022, p. 758). Luis, from Portugal, told a story about the necessity of merging diversity with inclusion:

> I was in one of the biggest social entrepreneurship conventions worldwide. And this time they made, for the first time, one panel. They have panels around many different topics related with social entrepreneurship. And they made one around accessibility and inclusion. And I said, 'whoa, this is incredible.'

But once he got there, Luis had mixed feelings:

> Of course, it's cool that they do the panel and it's cool that people talk about this topic and the panel is there. But there were ten people in the room only. And ... they all were social entrepreneurs like us who work in disability. For example, there was one person from a company, but her son was a disabled kid. In the end, 'Where is all the rest of the world?'

At the same time, managing a complex stakeholder landscape of both 'insiders' and 'outsiders' needs stewards, or what Vroom and Jago (1974) typologized as 'chairman' to make things happen in order for the change to be thorough enough to remain independently of the people involved at the time. This type of responsible stakeholder practice discussed in Chapter 2 is key to generating social capital through any inclusion project. Bernard, again, had his views on this:

> It is really important that they were part of the process from point A to point Z. So even if they are the ones benefiting from the program, they should be the ones implementing it and by taking ownership and responsibility this means that they're gonna really own the program. They're gonna participate much more. They're gonna enjoy it much more They're gonna recommend it much more. And then the outcomes and outputs of this program will be much, much bigger and much more important and positive.

This quote illustrates that by addressing social inclusion more broadly, and operationalizing it as a form of roundtable discussions, the ideals of representativeness through inclusive leadership can be a source of change towards increased access to otherwise closed-off facilities, processes, and stakeholders. In fact, the definition of social inclusion and exclusion by the Council of the European Union cited in Chapter 1 continues by emphasizing that social exclusion is a risk when people lack 'access to power and decision-making bodies and thus often feeling powerless and unable to take control over the decisions that affect their day to day lives' (Council of the European Union, 2003, p. 9). Similarly, a UN report claims that 'social exclusion entails not only material deprivation but also lack of agency or control over important decisions as well as feelings of alienation and inferiority' (UNDESA, 2010, p. 18).

Meanwhile, we share the view of Simmons and Yawson (2022) that inclusion and consensus are not the same, or that

> using inclusion to accomplish desired ends does not mean everyone has to be involved and every idea accepted. An important responsibility of leaders is to find out who really needs to be included. Involving everyone and every perspective results in death by over-collaboration.
> (p. 252)

Nina saw the solution to this as a strategic choice by leaders and recalled 'a life changing advice' by the CEO of the Munich Olympia Park in Germany:

> She came to me afterwards, introducing herself to me. And she said she makes a case of doing that, to introduce herself to younger females in events. So that there could be this support system among women as well, because they're so rare. And then I've tried to make sure that I do that myself. Or, you know, if there's younger female speakers in events where I tend to introduce myself, make the connection, praise them on their intervention.

By contrast, Bernard's solution to this was more diplomacy to address the conditions of complexity we discussed in Chapter 2:

> To sort of manage the competing interests that will occur in these kind of co-creation processes…I mean what if you use a metaphor, you have the gravity center. That's moving because everyone has their own interest as you mentioned, but the question is like, how do we compromise? I feel, like, just the process in itself to put people around the table if even if that creates complexity. Complexity is here anyway, so if you don't listen to these people complexity will remain but it will be untouched and it will be like buried and that's even worse.

While the risk with Nina's solution is to miss out on the people in need of being involved, as they are not always there in the first place, the downside with a diplomacy approach is that it is very time-consuming and not always on the agenda for leaders in sport organizations. One reason may be that the money holders are prioritizing competitive sports or have a funding model which is linked to elite performance. However, according to Sebastian, from Sweden, financial excuses were often a result of lack of knowledge, rather than lack of resources or priorities:

> It doesn't have to be a contradiction. These points do not work against each other. One should not necessarily exclude the other. And the only reason it does so, I think, is about knowledge issues ….you are not aware of what support and what opportunities…that's when you start dividing against each other when you say we have other problems or things we want to work on.

Bernard also acknowledged the challenges with his approach:

> I think that there are many shocks, if you call them like that, whether it's between policymakers, businesses, citizens, not for profit organizations, but there is one also in between like cultural backgrounds like

proper cultures of people and their education. There is a clash in between generations. I mean like there are many clashes that you can imagine. And that's the beauty of human beings and like different groups and different backgrounds, but that's a complexity we need to embrace.

In the next phase, however, when those in power are to be selecting the ones to be included in these roundtable discussions, things get more complicated. What is more, while it must be recognized that those who are typically excluded from sporting activities should be able to access sports facilities in order to participate in the activities on offer, 'this has been shown to be an unrealistic assumption for those who have been traditionally marginalized' (Waring & Mason, 2010, p. 526). For these reasons, positive discrimination, such as gender quotas, has been an important tool to improve female representation in sport leadership for almost two decades (Adriaanse, 2017). Often, from a social utility perspective, it is assumed that because there are 'gender differences in management styles, attitudes, experiences and interests,' an increasing presence of women 'in male-dominated leadership will promote new perspectives and ways of solving problems, which will result in higher productivity and a better working environment' (Muriaas & Peters, 2024, p. 5). Be that as it may, for social inclusion projects, where structural disadvantages are often present from the start, in addition to having to consider multiple group membership criteria (like gender, ethnicity, or age) simultaneously, decisions must be made on a different weighing of factors from those in an organization. In other words: who deserves attention from the sport club to be considered as the target group for a social inclusion project?

Making a difference by differentiating?

In order to answer the question ending the previous section, some point to the use of positive discrimination beyond categories to the entire project design and motive (Cano-Hila, 2022). As an example, Kunz et al. (2021) explain why one must have two thoughts at the same time:

> Initiatives that target a specific group are in fact not very integrative as such. However, it might be necessary to start with exclusive, tailored support for a specific target group in order to enable the participants to take part in the regular sports activities.
>
> (p. 18)

Sabine, from France, thought this argument 'necessary' to challenge the dominant culture:

Those projects are important because for some individuals, that's the only way. And they do identify in the group and that's the only way for them to have access, let's say, to sport activity at all. Because otherwise, if not through that group, they would never join any, they would never practice any physical activity or they would never be involved even interested or they would be too scared of joining a club or something.

The downside to positive discrimination is that the pendulum might swing the opposite way from what was intended. Discussing organizational inclusion, Adamson et al. (2021) underline that 'the term "inclusive" already carries a certain degree of ambivalence as inclusion may mean, for instance, submission to rules and hegemonic identity concepts' (p. 217). Instead of creating group belonging and appreciation of the group members' contribution to social progress, affirmative action may lead to less inclusion in society because of their group membership status. In workplace studies, one criticism related to this is that it negatively affects the organization, the ordinary employees, as well as the group members receiving preferential treatment (Noon, 2010). Criticizing the shortcomings of indicator culture in equality debates, Morgan et al. (2024, p. 1) found that 'the counting women paradigm contributes to forms of "non-knowledge" about women in sports organisations, flattening the ability to understand and address barriers to women's inclusion in sports leadership.'

Relatedly, in social inclusion projects, the benefits of being specific about target groups must be weighed against potential drawbacks of reinforcing a group identity people may have a conflicted relationship with. Lessard (2017) found that political support for local social inclusion projects adopted as a premise eschewing group targeting to avoid further negative discrimination and instead opted for a 'sport for all' approach. A study of LGBTQ+ athletes in Italian grassroots sports draws an even clearer picture of the situation. On the one hand, athletes had access to activity facilities, with 59% of the sample reporting being active in sport (marginally lower than EU as a whole, at 63%). On the other hand, they also reported numerous instances of homo- and trans-negativity, for example through derogatory language and verbal insults. Combined with a lack of legal protection against discrimination on the grounds of sexual orientation and gender identity, the efforts to resolve these issues have been hampered, or the problem has even increased, by political fluctuations towards the right and more conservative values (Heusslein et al., 2022).

Accordingly, by favouring positive discrimination in the context of access, clarification of the role of social exclusion is necessary. Looking at the European context, the Future ++ report underlines that while 'sport is not intrinsically educational or inclusive,' any intervention on any level 'must be accompanied by a true socio-educational and inclusive will' (Future ++, 2020, p. 20). For leaders, as emphasized by Nishii and Leroy (2022), this dynamic is inescapable and realizing this 'inclusive will' can hardly be done by being neutral. Rather, by being neutral, 'leaders perpetuate unequal societal structures that demand assimilation among those with non-dominant identities' (p. 690). Even more so, by acknowledging social identity differences and thereby strengthening uniqueness, neutrality may have an unintended consequence of reinforcing stereotypes, hence reducing people's autonomy (Nishii & Leroy, 2022, p. 690). As an example, Nicolai, a Danish informant working on many international social inclusion projects, was clear about using the organizational status to make a European stand when collaborating with organizations in what he referred to as Arab countries:

> I speak from my cultural point of view. And it is, after all, more Western European, and they know that. And I think they've had that too, they know well what Western European culture is like, they know what the difference is, so it's going very well. [To meetings] we send a woman when it's an Arab country on purpose. And it is also a signal.

In other words, paraphrasing the conceptual difference between the dimensions of inclusion discussed in Chapter 2, one must ask: by including a group in a smaller community, are you simultaneously categorizing them as a group in society and thus exposing them to exclusionary processes? While some refer to positive discrimination as the place to start, others point at society. It is argued that in recasting 'access to involve transformative action,' disability concerns are 'not simply a matter of individual inclusion but also a principal concern of social justice' (Bennett & Hannah, 2022, p. 328; see also Chapter 4). In connection with this, Aila said that with reference to her work as coordinator of social inclusion themes among clubs:

> I think it can be really sometimes easy for clubs to recruit people, but really for them to stay, I think that's the first phase when the inclusion really happens. Do they feel welcome? Do they feel safe to stay? Do they feel that they are really a part of the group? So, yes, I think there is really the key thing to really hear these people, the new people, how they feel, what they think. And maybe also to make other people, for example, in our organizations, encourage them to be open and including and what does it in practical means that it's not just one person, it's the whole organization …taking them on.

48 Sport, Leadership, and Social Inclusion

For Nina, this was a troublesome topic. Speaking about physical activity more generally rather than organized sports, both the wording and the content of any project could cause it to potentially miss the target:

> How do you make sure that you fulfill the needs of the target group in a way that is suitable for them? Because sometimes they might have very specific needs like Muslim women, for example. But you also want to make sure that the social inclusion integration happens. So that is it the question that we need to include them into our mainstream activities? Or is it rather that we need to be more diverse and open to accept diversity as it is? Or is it really an assimilation into Danish society or Norwegian society? Or can we exist in this cultural plurality? Yes, that's something that I struggle with existentially a lot.

Seemingly, the question of how to make access a part of social inclusion projects boils down to making the fit between needs, offers, and coordinating forces as good as possible. But to do so, a lot of groundwork is required, in addition to the demands on the organizations to follow up on the implemented activities. Judging from the overall impression of our informants on leadership in sport, being a leader in a sport organization today is a far cry from the management archetypes called 'Kitchen Table,' 'Boardroom,' and 'Executive Office' identified in the early 1990s (Kikulis et al., 1992). Rather, as discussed in Chapter 2, to flesh out what Barth called 'interests' and 'values' as sources of interactional choices and related to stakeholder considerations and decision-making, we must consider what Sewell (1992) said in his critique of Giddens' (1986) attempt to explain what constitutes agency: people don't relate to only one structure at the time because 'societies are based on practices that derive from many distinct structures, which exist at different levels, operate in different modalities, and are themselves based on widely varying types and quantities of resources' (Sewell, 1992, p. 16).

This finding raises the question of how decisions can be made to the best benefit of the representative population. A methodological shortcoming of Vroom and Jago's model for decision-making was that the study used 'a standardized set of administrative problems or cases, each of which depicted a leader faced with some organizational requirement for action or decision making' (Vroom & Jago, 1974, p. 767). By contrast, in sport, the leadership role, resources, and mission among those involved in social inclusion projects differ quite substantially. Standards do not exist and yet everybody strives towards the same sky, thus making constructive controversy (Tjosvold et al., 1986) unavoidable. As exemplified by the informants cited in this chapter, this 'race to the top' for the good of society between policy-makers and sport clubs, to put it simply, does not come cheap, without conflicts, or with fixed answers. Sporting democracies are sometimes prettier in name than in practice. In some cases, as underlined by Sabine, people resist becoming tokens of social inclusion because the burden is too heavy:

> Okay, 'you're part of a discriminated group, but we need you and you have to help us'….I mean, it's important to do it, and it's important to make the space to hear those voices, but we should also never undermine that it's okay if someone says no, because we're adding an extra burden on a situation that's sometimes already complicated to deal with.

This burden can come in different shapes. For example, even if a person belongs to a minority group, he/she cannot speak for all individuals with minority backgrounds. Furthermore, minority statuses often contain more diversity than the label accounts for. Studying the relationship between participation levels in organized sport, minority status, gender, and socio-economic background in Norway, Strandbu et al. (2019) found that while 'affiliation with Islam reduces the likelihood of sports participation among minority girls, this is not the case for boys' (p. 616). Put in a social inclusion setting, this multiple consideration matrix creates demands on leaders to be aware and knowledgeable (or collaborating with someone who is) of societal issues, trends, and winds defining 'access' in all its complexity. A summary of this argument is presented in Table 3.1. The challenge from a complexity leadership theory (CLT) perspective is

Table 3.1 Practical perspectives on access and social inclusion

	Understood as	*Operationalized through*	*Facilitated by*
Access	Physical	Material equality measures	Democratic use of sporting facilities Non-biased information about possibilities for socially inclusive activities in sport Objective indicators about social exclusion
	Political	Decision-making procedures	Inclusive agenda-setting Representational fairness Charting those not usually in the loop
	Socio-cultural	Differentiation strategies	Non-neutral leadership Group-targeting incentives Assessment of societal risks for re-stigmatization

that 'access,' as unpacked in this chapter, merely conditions how inclusion may be used in sport for specific purposes. If these expectations are to be upheld, the organization of sport needs to be rigged accordingly, with people in designated leadership roles who are able to facilitate questions of access like the ones discussed in this chapter. Thence, the three types of leadership posed by CLT theorists are warranted, as 'access' integrates various facets of societal complexity. To get one step further, we thus need to explore the next dimension of inclusion, which is participation.

Concluding remarks

In this chapter, we have found that access is a term with much more layers than both the neo-liberal understanding of it and the description used by EMS allows for. However, these layers can be merged or balanced by leaders if they exploit their role to make fair decisions possible. Rather than focusing on what type of decisions leaders make, or the decisions themselves, our analysis indicates that an essential component of facilitating access for social inclusion purposes is that leaders ensure stakeholder representativeness. Notwithstanding the importance of socio-economic variables or the physical shortage of activity facilities, the logic of realizing a social inclusion project is both similar to, and different from, ordinary sporting activities. Our discussion of access-related topics underpins Cano-Hila's (2022) argument that it is 'imperative to address the conditions under which people are/feel included, and how a claim and focus on universalism does not make differential treatment unworthy or stigmatizing' (p. 2).

This finding makes it necessary for leaders to abandon a neutral approach and instead tailor the justification of having this group or that project using the facilities in competition with everybody else (especially public facilities) towards other stakeholders' interests and aims. Particularly, the relationship between differentiating and equalizing efforts must be considered in the early phases of social inclusion projects as they influence the implementation of participation and empowerment. Although most of our informants do not separate aim from process or goal, the former is important for funding purposes. For operative measures, the process takes centre stage. For harnessing political goodwill, the goal is dominant. In between these notions of social inclusion, gathering information and insight on access-related issues is not always a matter of considering rational arguments or objective measures. Often, as with sport in general, it involves a lot of emotions and opinions in society mixed with formal requests and the need for advocacy through bureaucratic procedures with which for example children or migrants might be unfamiliar.

We will return to how this premise for societal value creation can blossom into participatory self-efficacy and empowering developments in the next chapters. But for those of us who are in a privileged position in society in general, it is vital to accept from the get-go the minority's desire to be acknowledged in decision-making processes as a premise for facilitating discussion on what is to be accessed and for what purpose. Tjosvold et al.'s (1986) suggestion to include 'constructive controversy' in the analysis requires organizational acceptance of the benefits of not shying away from disagreements. Above, we identified a need for an alternative for leaders to being neutral in access-related debates, as neutrality may reproduce power structures and overlook subtle norm differences which negatively affect those who are not among the dominant majority (Nishii & Leroy, 2022). Whereas the first step to achieving this is 'seeing who's not in the room,' the next step is how leaders can transform the achievement of getting access to something matched by real participatory means and opportunities.

References

Adamson, M., Kelan, E., Lewis, P., Śliwa, M., & Rumens, N. (2021). Introduction: Critically interrogating inclusion in organisations. *Organization*, *28*(2), 211–227. https://doi.org/10.1177/1350508420973307

Adriaanse, J. A. (2017). Quotas to accelerate gender equity in sport leadership: Do they work? In S. Leberman, & L. J. Burton (eds.), *Women in sport leadership. Research and practice for change* (pp. 83–97). Routledge.

Barth, F. (1972). Analytical dimensions in the comparison of social organizations. *American Anthropologist*, *74*(1/2), 207–220. https://doi.org/10.1525/aa.1972.74.1-2.02a01720

Bennett, K. C., & Hannah, M. A. (2022). Transforming the rights-based encounter: Disability rights, disability justice, and the ethics of access. *Journal of Business and Technical Communication*, *36*(3), 326–354. https://doi.org/10.1177/10506519221087960

Bergsgaard, N. A. (2017). Spillet om idrettsanleggene – hvilke ressurser er virksomme ilokale anleggsprosesser? [The sports facility game – What resources are active in local facility processes?] *Norsk sosiologisk tidsskrift*, [*The Norwegian Journal of Sociology*], *1*(2), 171–187. https://doi.org/10.18261/issn.2535-2512-2017-02-05

By, R. T. (2021). Leadership: In pursuit of purpose. *Journal of Change Management*, *21*(1), 30–44. https://doi.org/10.1080/14697017.2021.1861698

Cano-Hila, A. (2022). Understanding social inclusion in contemporary society: Challenges, reflections, limitations, and proposals. *Social Inclusion*, *10*(2), 1–5. https://doi.org/10.17645/si.v10i2.5090

Cass, N., Shove, E., & Urry, J. (2005). Social exclusion, mobility and access. *The Sociological Review*, *53*(3), 539–555. https://doi.org/10.1111/j.1467-954X.2005.00565.x

Cochrane, T., & Davey, R. C. (2008). Increasing uptake of physical activity: A social ecological approach. *Journal of the Royal Society for the Promotion of Health*, *128*, 31–40.

Council of the European Union (2003). *Joint Report by the Commission and the Council on Social Inclusion*. Council of the European Union. http://ec.europa.eu/employment_social/soc-prot/soc-incl/final_joint_inclusion_report_2003_en.pdf. Accessed 12 July 2017.

Dugarova, E. (2015). *Social inclusion, poverty eradication and the 2030 agenda for sustainable development. UNRISD Working Paper, No. 2015-15*, United Nations Research Institute for Social Development (UNRISD), Geneva. https://www.econstor.eu/bitstream/10419/148736/1/861278364.pdf

European Commission (2021). *Mapping of innovative practices in the EU to promote sport outside of traditional structures – Final report to the European Commission*, Directorate-General for Education, Youth, Sport and Culture, Publications Office. https://doi.org/10.2766/063092

Fehsenfeld, M. (2015). Inclusion of outsiders through sport. *Physical Culture and Sport Studies and Research, 65*(1), 31–40. https://doi.org/10.1515/pcssr-2015-0009

Future ++ (2020). *Future ++ handbook. Sport and social inclusion: Future for children++*. https://future2plus.eu/wp-content/uploads/2023/12/FUTURE-HANDBOOK-ENGLISH-VERSION.pdf

Giddens, A. (1986). *The constitution of society*. Oxford University Press.

Gidley, J., Hampson, G., Wheeler, L., & Bereded-Samuel, E. (2010). Social inclusion: Context, theory and practice. *The Australasian Journal of University-Community Engagement, 5*(1), 6–36.

Hallmann, K., Wicker, P., Breuer, C., & Schönherr, L. (2012). Understanding the importance of sport infrastructure for participation in different sports – Findings from multi-level modeling. *European Sport Management Quarterly, 12*(5), 525–544. https://doi.org/10.1080/16184742.2012.687756

Heusslein, K., Coco, R., & Bibbiani, I. (2022). Inclusion policy and the experiences of LGBTQ+ athletes in grassroot sports in Italy. In I. Hartmann-Tews (ed.), *Sport, identity and inclusion in Europe. The experiences of LGBTQ+ people in sport* (pp. 104–115). Routledge.

Jones, M. (2010). Inclusion, social inclusion and participation. In M. H. Rioux, L. A. Basser, & M. Jones (eds.), *Critical perspectives on human rights and disability law* (pp. 57–82). Brill. https://doi.org/10.1163/ej.9789004189508.i-552.24

Kikulis, L. M., Slack, T., & Hinings, C. R. (1992). Institutionally specific design archetypes: A framework for understanding change in national sports organizations. *International Review for the Sociology of Sport, 27*(4), 343–368. https://doi.org/10.1177/101269029202700405

Kung, S. P., & Taylor, P. (2014). The use of public sports facilities by the disabled in England. *Sport Management Review, 17*(1), 8–22. https://doi.org/10.1016/j.smr.2013.08.009

Kunz, A., Meier, I., Nicoletti, I., Philipp, S., & Star, K. (2021). *The toolkit for equality. City policies against racism*. ETC Graz. https://www.eccar.info/sites/default/files/document/12_Toolkit-en-Sports.pdf

Lessard, C. (2017). Sport et prévention de la délinquance. Représentations et implications des acteurs municipaux de six communes d'Île-de-France. *Sciences sociales et sport*, *10*, 51–78. https://doi.org/10.3917/rsss.010.0051

Liu, Y. D., Taylor, P., & Shibli, S. (2008). Sport equity: Benchmarking the performance of English public sport facilities. *European Sport Management Quarterly*, *9*(1), 3–21. https://doi.org/10.1080/16184740802461686

Morgan, T., Henne, K., Blacklock, J., & Starre, K. (2024). Counting women: Indicator culture and gender inclusion in sports leadership. *International Review for the Sociology of Sport*. https://doi.org/10.1177/10126902241297882

Muriaas, R. L., & Peters, Y. (2024). Attitudes to gender quotas: Why and where to adjust gender imbalance in leadership. *European Journal of Political Research*. https://doi.org/10.1111/1475-6765.12680

Næss, H. E., & Svendsen, M. (2024). "We are not selling soap here, you know": Eight humanistic leadership qualities in sport. *Leadership*, *20*(3), 144–161. https://doi.org/10.1177/17427150241237925

Nishii, L. H., & Leroy, H. (2022). A multi-level framework of inclusive leadership in organizations. *Group & Organization Management*, *47*(4), 683–722. https://doi.org/10.1177/10596011221111505

Noon, M. (2010). The shackled runner: Time to rethink positive discrimination? *Work, Employment and Society*, *24*(4), 728–739. https://doi.org/10.1177/0950017010380648

Pedras, L., Taylor, T., & Frawley, S. (2020). Responses to multi-level institutional complexity in a national sport federation. *Sport Management Review*, *23*(3), 482–497, https://doi.org/10.1016/j.smr.2019.05.001

Persson, M., Espedalen, L. E., Stefansen, K., & Strandbu, Å. (2020). Opting out of youth sports: How can we understand the social processes involved? *Sport, Education and Society*, *25*(7), 842–854. https://doi.org/10.1080/13573322.2019.1663811

Pot, N., Verbeek, J., van der Zwan, J., & van Hilvoorde, I. (2016). Socialisation into organised sports of young adolescents with a lower socio-economic status. *Sport, Education and Society*, *21*(3), 319–338. https://doi.org/10.1080/13573322.2014.914901

Richard, V., Piumatti, G., Pullen, N., et al. (2023). Socioeconomic inequalities in sport participation: Pattern per sport and time trends – a repeated cross-sectional study. *BMC Public Health*, *23*, 785. https://doi.org/10.1186/s12889-023-15650-7

Roberson, Q., & Perry, J. L. (2022). Inclusive leadership in thought and action: A thematic analysis. *Group & Organization Management*, *47*(4), 755–778. https://doi.org/10.1177/10596011211013161

Sewell, W. H. (1992). A theory of structure: Duality, agency, and transformation. *American Journal of Sociology*, *98*(1), 1–29. https://doi.org/10.1086/229967

Simmons, S. V., & Yawson, R. M. (2022). Developing leaders for disruptive change: An inclusive leadership approach. *Advances in Developing*

Human Resources, 24(4), 242–262. https://doi.org/10.1177/152342 23221114359

Somerset, S. & Hoare, D. J. (2018). Barriers to voluntary participation in sport for children: A systematic review. *BMC Pediatrics*, 18(1). https://doi.org/10.1186/s12887-018-1014-1V

Strandbu, Å., Bakken, A., & Sletten, M. A. (2019). Exploring the minority–majority gap in sport participation: Different patterns for boys and girls?, *Sport in Society*, 22(4), 606–624, https://doi.org/10.1080/17430437.2017.1389056

Tjosvold, D., Wedley, W. C., & Richard H. G. Field. (1986). Constructive controversy, the Vroom-Yetton model, and managerial decision-making. *Journal of Occupational Behaviour*, 7(2), 125–138. https://doi.org/10.1002/job.4030070205

Uhl-Bien, M., & Marion, R. (2009). Complexity leadership in bureaucratic forms of organizing: A meso model. *The Leadership Quarterly*, 20, 631–650. https://doi.org/10.1016/j.leaqua.2009.04.007

UNDESA (2010). *Analysing and measuring social inclusion in a global context*. A study prepared by Anthony B. Atkinson and Eric Marlier. UN. https://www.un.org/esa/socdev/publications/measuring-social-inclusion.pdf

Vroom, V. H., & Jago, A. G. (1974). Decision-making as a social process: Normative and descriptive models of leader behavior. *Decision Sciences*, 5, 743–769. https://doi.org/10.1111/j.1540-5915.1974.tb00651.x

Vroom, V. H., & Jago, A. G. (1978). On the validity of the Vroom-Yetton model. *Journal of Applied Psychology*, 63(2), 151–162. https://doi.org/10.1037/0021-9010.63.2.151

Waring, A., & Mason, C. (2010). Opening doors: Promoting social inclusion through increased sports opportunities. *Sport in Society*, 13(3), 517–529. https://doi.org/10.1080/17430431003588192

4 The role of leadership in facilitating participation

Introduction

The second dimension of the social inclusion model by Gidley et al. (2010a) is participation. Participation in sport can refer to simply taking part in an activity. As such the concept is often used interchangeably with access, as described in Chapter 3 (Lange et al., 2024). Yet a different understanding of participation is concerned with the degree of influence experienced when taking part in an activity (Heller, 2003). In this chapter, our focus is on the latter view as simply participating in a sport activity, does not necessarily lead to social inclusion or empowerment, as will be discussed in more depth in Chapter 5. Chapter 3 concluded by underlining the importance of identifying 'who is not at the table.' However, in this chapter we will focus on what happens when people vulnerable to exclusion are actually sitting at the table, trying to influence matters that are important to them. Understanding participation as a concept related to influence, Gidley et al. (2010a) argue that seeing social inclusion as participation, in this sense, provides a more comprehensive understanding of social inclusion, and that the concept is connected to social justice ideology. They argue that:

> from the perspective of social justice ideologies, increasing social inclusion is about human rights, egalitarianism of opportunity, human dignity, and fairness for all. It may or may not be linked to economic interests, but its primary aim is to enable all human beings to participate fully in society with respect for their human dignity. Here, acts of community engagement and participation are foregrounded.
>
> (p. 10)

Thus, whereas access is necessary for social inclusion to occur, it should be considered merely as a starting point. As exemplified by Liu (2009), certain groups in society are significantly underrepresented, although they have access to the same facilities. Likewise, Mutz and Müller (2021) find in their comparison of ten sport activities that taking part in sport is socially stratified. Connecting this research to Gidley et al.'s (2010a, 2010b) understanding of participation, these findings may imply a lack of voice from certain groups in society and raise the question of whether more people would participate in sport if they were invited to on their own terms and with their own needs and wishes being met. This leads us to the main research question of this chapter which is to explore what leaders can do to facilitate social inclusion through participation in sport?

To illuminate this research question, the chapter will proceed as follows. First, we discuss the multifaceted concept of participation in a social inclusion context. As a consequence of what we derive from this discussion, the concept of participation will be specified by referring to social justice theory rationalized by the claim that 'social justice interpretations of social inclusion comprise complex integrations involving participatory dialogue arising from the full ecology of interests regardless of power' (Gidley et al., 2010b, p. 11). Moving forward, we analyse how the intricacies of power sharing must be considered for participation in a social justice framework to take place. To rectify the current power sharing deficiencies, we argue that addressing boundary conditions for participation is necessary because operationalizing social inclusion beyond access requires allowing people to voice their interest, concerns, and standpoints, to learn about the sporting setting and eventually to challenge its exclusionary features. Along the way, examples from our sample of leaders will be extensively used, before the chapter ends with some practical considerations and concluding remarks.

The many facets of participation

Participation is a multifaceted concept that has historically lacked clarity and consistency in its application. At its core, participation involves individuals influencing matters that are important to them, whether through direct engagement or indirect representation (Gallie, 2013). However, the meaning and implementation of participation can vary widely depending on the context, often leading to ambiguity. As highlighted by Gidley et al. (2010a), to feel that you are participating fully, on your own terms and engaged in something, it is pivotal that you experience that your voice is being heard. Yet, the narratives of the dominant, privileged groups tend to dominate society and sport is no exception (Foucault, 2013; Harris & Adams, 2016). This is also pinpointed by Kidd

(2008) who asserts that a problem with social inclusion through sport for development initiatives is:

> 'top down' control. Whereas the best community development is 'needs- and asset-based', i.e. premised on the expressed needs and available resources of the local population, articulated during a careful, consultative joint planning process, much of SDP is donor-defined, planned and conducted with missionary zeal.
>
> (p. 377)

As such, it seems that if participatory practices are lacking, sport may not be able to increase the feeling of influence (or empowerment as will be further discussed in Chapter 5) regardless of the access to opportunities facing the individual discussed in Chapter 3. The *essence* of participation is illustrated by our informant Bernard from France who explains:

> It's a bit like diplomacy. It's about asking: What do you want? What do I want? Then we find a middle ground. When everything is on the table, and we have a clear map of all your needs and wants, even if the center of gravity isn't exactly where you stand, I can always refer back to that map over time. I can say, 'Oh, you also wanted ABC, which isn't included here, but I'm aware of it.' This way, everything is transparent and clear, and we can adapt as we evolve.

The *importance* of participation for social inclusion in the broader society is highlighted by Aila from Finland who explains that:

> polarization is what is happening in our society when we are not listening to each other and trying to understand…what I really see is important…is to create this kind of safe space where people who have these different views, …feel safe and able to discuss these topics. And maybe in some cases it comes up that we have the same actual values, but we are just expressing them in different ways.

Bernard's and Aila's examples highlight the complexities of participation, demonstrating that simply inviting the right people to the table is not enough. Although removing barriers to access is necessary, as discussed in Chapter 3, it is not sufficient to make a lasting change. Around the table, meaningful processes – such as compromise, negotiation, and information sharing – must take place for true participation to occur. For these processes to succeed, leaders must address the social complexities of inclusion, as outlined in Chapter 2, and empathetically connect with the diverse groups vulnerable to exclusion. Alexandra from Norway illustrated this challenge in a conversation with a senior leader in a federation, who, like herself, also had a minority background. They discussed the troubling reality of having so few individuals from minority backgrounds represented within the federation. Alexandra explained that:

> they don't understand, they don't see what they're doing, and that's because when you've never been different or wrong, then you don't understand, so you can't recognize it either. When [the federation] is criticized for having mostly just a bunch of yes-men working in the central management, they perceive it as unreasonable and unfair criticism. They don't see that it obviously creates blind spots that they can't identify. Because they haven't been there themselves.

Alexandra, however, is quick to highlight that this is not because of bad character, but rather low awareness;

> It's not because they are bad people, it's not because they are dumb, or because they are racist, or because they are mean, or because of anything at all. What they lack is experience, and they are not willing to acknowledge that competence…. And so, Norwegian sports at the top lack competence in quite a few things. And that's because many of those who work there, well, in the past, they were athletes, and now, this is anonymous, so I can say to you, now it's just a bunch of idiots who know about digitization and commercialization. It's like, what the fuck, you know nothing about the damn legislation you're supposed to deal with.

For the participants in sports themselves, however, Alexandra neatly illustrated how individuals from marginalized groups are not participating because they are simply not invited:

> Sports have been really good at that, pointing at minority parents and saying they're not interested, they're not willing, right? Or at women, they don't have ambition, or they don't think it's important, or they can't be bothered, right? And then you have to shift the focus to the organization and see who is being invited in as volunteers, who is being asked.

Alexandra concludes that 'those who are not thriving today, the main reason is that, most say that they have never been asked.' To sum up, participation is a complex concept that involves more than just including people; it requires genuine efforts to listen, engage, and uplift marginalized groups. It has become evident that sports may even perpetuate exclusion through top-down approaches and insufficient participatory practices, emphasizing the need for empathy, negotiation, and inclusive processes. As such, it becomes clear that participation is connected to power.

Actual participation requires the sharing of power

Our leaders illustrated the many ways in which participation is linked to the distribution of power. In contrast to the neo-liberal perspective, social justice theory has shaped our understanding of social inclusion in sport by emphasizing how the voices of marginalized groups – often the focus of sport-based inclusion initiatives – are overlooked or ignored. This leads to the dominance of privileged narratives and the suppression of alternative perspectives (Nicholls et al., 2010). Alexandra said that:

> It's about the right to be a valuable member of the community. It means that you have the right to be heard, but it doesn't mean that you have the right to have people agree with you. Right? And you have the right to be taken seriously, you have the right to be acknowledged from your standpoint.

Alexandras's quote is one example of how participation in sport is intertwined with power dynamics. The importance of power dynamics is acknowledged by Kidd (2008) who calls for research that examines the challenges of sport participation to 'add to our growing knowledge of the precise circumstances under which sport may result in positive outcomes for gender relations, disability inclusion, youth development, mental health, peace and conflict resolution … for different populations and individuals' (p. 377). Responding to this call, Darnell and Millington (2018), conclude in their theoretical analysis of social inclusion through sport initiatives, that:

> the pursuit of social justice is a fundamentally different approach and project than using the popularity of sport to bestow charitable benefits on the poor and marginalized, or to use the "lessons" of sport to teach people to survive amidst inequality.
>
> (p. 176)

Hence, to apply the lens of social justice may get us further in grasping the complexity of social inclusion in sport. According to a review by Khechen (2013), participation in the context of social justice means individuals are given a chance to participate in decisions that govern their lives. This includes 'not only engaging them in deciding on the kind of public services needed in their areas but also ensuring their full participation in political and cultural life' (p. 5). Based on Rawls' social justice theory, Khechen (2013) argues that participation alters existing power relations and 'strengthens the position of traditionally weak and marginalized groups and individuals vis-à-vis other such actors as public and social institutions' (p. 5). This point sits well with Knudsen et al.'s (2011) view of participation as a continuum ranging from no control over decisions being made, to receiving information, joint consultation, joint decision-making and full control over the decisions being made. The importance, but also the difficulties of reaching the right side of this continuum, is expressed by Alise from Lithuania. She explains how she understands social inclusion in three steps. The first step is raising awareness. An example of this is a program they initiated to make people from different sport organizations become better at making activities more adaptable for different kinds of disabilities, refugees, and disadvantaged backgrounds. The second step, according to Alise, is when you include people with disabilities in activities. The third step, however, is related to power and the actual sharing of influence. She explains that;

> The third step would be where people with disabilities or let's say inclusion in general, they lead the activity so they are the ones who becoming the leaders. I think for the third step we are still struggling because we rarely have in our activities a concrete projects where people with disabilities or disadvantaged backgrounds or LGBTQ plus or refugees, the ones that they would be the ones leading the activities, being the trainers, being the facilitators, being, you know, the ones who are speakers and et cetera. So here, I also am very, very honest. This is our goal to get into that stage.

As exemplified by Alise, the level of participation taking place in an organization is related to power. Some theories have tended to view participation in a plus-sum perceptive, meaning that 'everyone can participate, and no one loses out' (Heller, 2003, p. 147). A result of this way of viewing participation is that it fails to acknowledge that, for real participation to occur, there must be a smaller or larger shift in influence or authority. As an example, which expands the discussion from Chapter 3, Karl from Austria highlights the importance of *representative* participation for social inclusion of minority groups. He explains that:

> Far more resources need to go to those who are affected by exclusion… maybe the minorities and vulnerable groups are then more in the center. They would be in the committees; they would be in where or nearer where the decisions would be taken. And that probably would change also some of the cultural things in sport that it's not having this. You know, the expression, the white elder male…

As such, participation is always part of a larger political power system and will often be resisted by people who fear that it will undermine their own position (Heller, 2003). Sabine, from France, tells us that people have the feeling that they have been fighting all their life to be in leadership positions, and therefore see diversity and social inclusion as a threat. She contends that:

> Many sport leaders like the concept of being democratic, universal, inclusive, and all those values that they promote as a federation. But it's really contradicting behaviors, I guess, to maintain the position they're in. As soon as we were discussing opening up, maybe having some quotas, you know, trying to embrace a bit more diversity in the structure, everybody was … super positive, like, okay, we need to work on this. Of course, it's a super important topic. We can't, as an international federation, not work on these topics. So, 'great if you have those little projects going on here and there, as long as I'm not involved. And as long as it's not endangering my position.'

In addition, there is often a fixed number of 'seats' around the table where decisions are made. The fact that participation is often considered a zero-sum game in sport is highlighted by Nina from Estonia who states that:

> inclusive leadership is something where a lot of work needs to be done. And it seems to me that it's difficult for people in power to spread that power or let it go. So it's part of good governance in terms of limits, making sure that there are principles in place that would encourage inclusion at the highest leadership level.

A danger of viewing participation as a plus-sum game is that it may facilitate what Heller (2003) refers to as inauthentic or pseudo-participation, where people are invited to participate without real influence-sharing taking place. This lack of influence sharing is often legitimized by wanting to give individuals a feeling of power, with the aim to improve managerial satisfaction, to reduce resistance in situations where decisions have already been taken, or where there is no real intention to take the inputs that result from the consultations into account. As such, 'pseudo participation denotes management techniques, which, even though involving information and consultation of employees, aim at persuading employees to accept decisions that have already been taken' (Knudsen et al., 2011, p. 380). Pseudo-participation has its roots in the theoretical distinction between espoused and actual behaviour (Argyris, 1976). According to this theoretical stance, managers feel the need to espouse participation because it has become an expected part of being a leader, however, acting on it might endanger their managerial power. Pseudo-participation is often linked to a large degree of scepticism and frustration when encountered over time. People don't necessarily confront pseudo-participation directly, but they still respond by showing distrust (Heller, 2003).

Pseudo-participation can take many forms at different levels and in varying contexts in sport organizations. Nina recalled a story about attending a conference where she was in one of the two first panels that started the conference. Both panels were predominantly female on purpose, to show representation of women and give a chance to female voices. However, as the conference proceeded Nina recalled that:

> the organizers did an Instagram reel of the event. But they didn't show a single female speaker. So, in the communication, all of the speakers were male. …we commented on Instagram. And the next day, because I was still there and I had access to the speaker launch. And I went there, and I made a comment to them. And it's something very obvious. But it's maybe because the leadership was male.

Pseudo-participation may also take place in the implementation process at an organizational level. Aila gives an example where implementation is done for the sake of appearances and not because of a sincere interest in social inclusion:

> Hockey in Finland, which has really, I don't know, but it has really been accused the last year for racism. So I think that's also like even I think the problem is that even if they say that we are doing active measures, they are still not being implemented genuinely.

The challenge with pseudo-participation in relation to social inclusion also becomes evident when it comes to social inclusion through volunteering. Alise explains that:

> You know, you cannot carry bottled water or whatever all the time…. You need to have a real responsibility. We don't want to say, okay, you're going to, you know, making lines or carry the bottles or say welcome to the people when they enter the room. You want to give them real responsibility. So organizing, facilitating, managing the teams and etcetera.

The above examples highlight how pseudo-participation can occur in different levels in sport, and how it can have a detrimental influence on social inclusion. As such, Bernard highlights how harmful it is to not attend to these issues as:

> Expectations or needs can evolve and in that sense there is also a need for kind of a checking quite regularly. But to me, yeah, if you don't touch upon this topic, [it] is like ignoring and burying kind of the real

truth. And it means like building on false foundations that are very unstable and very dangerous as well.

Considering the necessity of power sharing to real social inclusion, we will now turn our attention to important barriers to participation in sport and discuss what leaders can do to help reduce some of them, to foster social inclusion through genuine participation in sport.

Boundary conditions of participation

Dachler and Wilpert (1978) argue that to effectively implement participatory arrangements, it is essential to identify both their limitations and opportunities, as well as the complex interdependencies they entail. Dachler and Wilpert emphasize several boundary conditions that shape the success of participatory efforts. In our analysis, three of their identified boundary conditions emerged as particularly central for fostering social inclusion through participation in sport: the social range of participation, the balance between formal and informal participation and the complexity of the decisions being addressed. These factors play a critical role in determining the effectiveness of participatory arrangements relating to social inclusion.

The first boundary condition is related to Dachler and Wilperts (1978) concept of social range, which is concerned with the range of people, divisions, and organizations involved in a participatory system. As such, a participatory system with limited social range will only consider the interests of some sub-groups, while others will be left out. Accordingly, a key component for increasing social inclusion through sport is to aim for a broad social range, as discussed in Chapter 3. A challenge to this aim is *time*. Listening to different views and taking varying interests and stakeholder views into account takes time. As such, participation leads to a plethora of contingencies, which sometimes make interpretation difficult and action impossible (Heller, 2003). Looking back at Chapter 3 where Vroom and Yetton's (Vroom & Jago, 1974) contingency theory of leadership was introduced, time constraints are underlined as one of three major factors that influence how leadership decisions should be made. According to the theory, participation in decision-making is different in diverse scenarios, and therefore leaders need to determine their leadership style, for example, consultative or autocratic, based on what is appropriate for the situation. For example, if speed is required, more autocratic processes will be effective, where the leader takes the decision alone. If collaboration is preferred, however, a more democratic process will be superior, where the leader acts as a facilitator. Time available for reaching a decision is thus decisive for the influence sharing of leaders. However, the theory also posits that the more time available, the better the quality of decisions that can be made (Vignesh, 2020). This point is acknowledged by Alexandra who explains that:

> A more feminine leadership style is more inclusive. Such things play a role, as one is, of course, influenced by them. For example, a Secretary General once told me that the meeting that the previous chair, who was a man, could conduct in 45 minutes, I can barely manage to conduct in three hours. And I just say, 'thank you very much, I take that as a compliment'. And that's because people get to say what's on their minds. And I believe that's important because I think the democratic aspect and the deliberative process have intrinsic value.

Time is often scarce in sport organizations, especially since much work that is done there is done by volunteers in addition to other work and family obligations. Yet, Vroom and Jago (1978) offer some perspectives on when and how influence sharing is necessary and efficient, and state that power sharing may be especially important if you a) need commitment from group members, b) if you need their competence on the issue at hand, and c) to reduce conflicting issues. Accordingly, influence sharing may be especially important with regard to social inclusion issues, considering how 'participation, that is to say influence and its distribution in an organization, is the way power engages with human capital' (Heller, 2003, p. 160). Hence, spending a considerable time on sharing influence on social inclusion issues, may be justified in relation to other priorities. Sharing decision-making is also an important part of inclusive leadership and an important way to foster belonging within a group (Veli Korkmaz et al., 2022). To conclude so far, however, it is sufficient to say that time is a considerable barrier to social inclusion through participation in sport. Nonetheless, in the paradox between time and efficiency, spending time on including more people in decisions and volunteer work, may be of importance for inclusion issues, as this concept is strongly connected to social capital. Characteristics found in collaborative leadership such as mentorship, constructive feedback provision, open sharing of data, strong network building skills and contextual intelligence are thus factors sports leaders should consider (Vignesh, 2020).

The second boundary condition is the nexus between formal and informal participation. While formal participation often involves being seen as worthy of a seat at the table (see Chapter 3), informal participation requires the use of voice – defined as the upward communication of ideas, suggestions, and concerns aimed at improving organizational functioning (Liang et al., 2012). However, expressing opinions, suggestions and concerns can be a risky endeavour (Detert & Burris, 2007). In this context, voice self-efficacy – the confidence and competence individuals possess in formulating and expressing their viewpoints – is essential for enabling effective self-expression (Yan et al., 2022). While we previously emphasized the importance of competency among leaders, this requirement is frequently overlooked when addressing efforts to increase participation in sports for marginalized groups (Heller, 2003). Alise explains that:

> You cannot go into the decision making without having a sufficient background and sufficient knowledge. It's not enough just to stand there and say, you know, I think it should be different. You have to have arguments and learn how to express your arguments. So this is also part of the trainings, what we do for different backgrounds, that it's not enough to have your opinion, you also need to know how to express it in the way that it would be listened to, how to advocate and also in an argumentative manner.

Yet having enough background and sufficient knowledge may not always be easy in sport and is very relatable to the way leaders and organizations are able to convey their information. Much of an organization's culture is hidden in, for example, gendered norms of 'the way we do things around here.' Reviewing the gender aspect of organizational dimensions, Piggott et al. (2024) found examples of these practices relating to dress code, informal socializing, and expectations towards leaders which are open to those in the know but invisible to others. Another study found that by reproducing a hegemonic view of gender inequities as natural, expected, or normal, the organization 'provided little space for dialogue about the serious nature of the inequities, the immediate need to address them, or a more comprehensive approach to implementing gender equity for athletes' (Hoeber, 2007, p. 275).

The third boundary condition pertains to content complexity, which refers to how a lack of knowledge and information presented in a way that is unsuitable for its audience becomes a significant barrier to participation. Alise explains that:

> the way we, as organizations and leaders, communicate about things – how easy it is to understand the structures or the work of the organization, or how someone can get involved – is not always clear. For individuals from diverse backgrounds, especially those involved in Special Olympics, the language must be super simple, super easy, and highly understandable. Yet, you open our documents, and you see 50-page reports, leaving people saying, 'OK, I have no idea what's in there.' So, yeah, I think that's also a big barrier.

Similarly, Alexandra tells us a story of how lack of cultural knowledge may hinder participation and volunteering among immigrant parents.

She explains that 'immigrant parents who have come to Norway, they have no idea how these organizations are organized. Because in very, very, very many countries in the world, for example, in school, it is the gym teacher who does the job.' Alexandra explains that parents of immigrants often feel uncomfortable stepping into roles that seem to encroach on the responsibilities of others, such as taking on tasks typically handled by a gym teacher. She also argues that Norwegian leaders frequently fail to understand or empathize with the perspectives of immigrant parents. To illustrate this point, Alexandra shares an analogy she often uses with Norwegian sport leaders to enhance their awareness and understanding of these dynamics:

> Imagine I go to the grocery store one day. I've had a quiet day at work, I'm in a good mood, full of energy, and considering whether to go for a run later. At the store, I notice there's a long queue at the checkout, and the atmosphere is stressful. I could, in theory, walk over and say, 'I'll just sit at register four to help out for an hour and get through the rush.' But, of course, I wouldn't do that – because I have no business being there. It would be completely absurd. That's how it can feel for immigrant parents when interacting with sports organizations. You don't just walk in and take over.

To reduce barriers to informal voice use and address feelings of inadequate competence or cultural knowledge, the concept of self-efficacy – defined as an individual's belief in their ability to successfully complete a task (Bandura, 1997) – emerges as particularly significant. Self-efficacy has been recognized as a critical factor in fostering participation within organizational contexts. For instance, Veiga (1991) concludes that individuals feeling they lack competence may reduce participatory behaviours in groups. Similarly, Heller (2019) highlights that feeling competent and having opportunities to apply this competence through participation can unleash motivational energy. The domain-specific concept of self-efficacy will be examined in greater depth in Chapter 5, particularly in relation to empowerment and its connection to life skills. However, this chapter focuses on the role of self-efficacy in relation to participation, particularly in the context of the boundary conditions identified by Dachler and Wilpert (1978). A central question therefore arises: what can sport leaders do to enhance self-efficacy related to participation among their members? First, according to socio-cognitive theory, the major way of fostering self-efficacy in individuals is through mastery experiences (Bandura, 1997, 2006). Mastery experiences come from the experience of success in doing a task. Conversely, consistent failures at a task may affect efficacy perceptions negatively. Leaders can play an important part in shaping individuals' perception of self-efficacy by creating arenas where individuals can express themselves. This is accomplished by being participative and by giving room for different opinions and recognizing people's efforts to express themselves (Tangirala & Ramanujam, 2012; Svendsen et al., 2016). The essence of participative leadership is exemplified by Alexandra who contends that:

> the goal should be to make disagreements visible, because it creates trust among those who don't agree with the majority. They might think, is there something wrong with me? Or does everyone think the same way? I don't want to be a part of that. But if you highlight disagreements and show a diversity of opinions, perspectives, and reflections, first of all, you will make much better decisions if everyone dares to speak up and feels it is their duty to bring forward different viewpoints.

Creating spaces for participation and signalling that it is acceptable to disagree can be challenging in sports contexts. This challenge is closely tied to the concept of psychological safety, understood as both an individual and group construct. Psychological safety refers to the perception of an environment as safe for interpersonal risk-taking (Kahn, 1990; Edmondson, 1999; Edmondson & Bransby, 2023). It involves the assurance that expressing oneself will not result in negative consequences, such as ridicule, ostracism, damage to one's professional or social network, or other sanctions (Kahn, 1990; Detert & Burris, 2007). Empirical research highlights the importance of psychological safety, particularly when addressing sensitive issues that carry greater personal risks for those speaking up (Svendsen et al., 2016). In this context, psychological safety is especially critical for participatory practices aimed at promoting social inclusion. Leaders play a key role in fostering psychologically safe environments, as they often control the distribution of rewards and sanctions (Liu et al., 2010). A leader who demonstrates approachability and shows appreciation when individuals share suggestions or concerns contributes significantly to the perception that self-expression will not lead to negative outcomes (Liang et al., 2012). Alexandra points out a critical challenge within sports organizations: the value of loyalty, as it is currently interpreted, can stifle openness to disagreement and impede organizational progress. She observes that loyalty is one of the core values in sports organizations, and while loyalty itself is not inherently problematic, its interpretation within the organizational culture is. Specifically, she argues that loyalty is often understood as unwavering agreement with those in positions of authority. When leaders make decisions or take a stance, there is an implicit expectation that everyone else must align with them. Disagreement, in this context, is perceived as disloyal, which creates a fear of speaking up. Specifically, Alexandra contends that:

It's not the value of loyalty that is the problem, it's the organizational culture that is the problem. People are terrified of exposing disagreement. And I don't understand that, but I think it's because it is a very homogenous group that thinks very similarly. And then disagreement becomes uncomfortable. But I say that what creates trust among the members is if we make our disagreements visible. If someone thought this way, and someone thought that way, it needs to be made visible to the members. Because that builds trust. It builds loyalty.

As such, participative leadership does not occur in a vacuum and needs to be supported by organizational values and structures in order to create proper arenas for psychological safety and self-efficacy so that individuals can have mastery experiences with participation and daring to express themselves. Heller (2003) argues that one of the reasons why many attempts to promote participatory practices in organizations fails is because we look at them in isolation, and don't take a holistic perspective that also includes organizational culture and structures. Trine from Norway highlights the fact that leadership is always embedded in organizational structures that, in turn, affects leadership's ability to influence inclusion issues:

One of the biggest problems is the ideal of the masculine leader, which favors men in Norwegian sports. What we see is that if you possess typically masculine traits or skills, you will be in a good position to climb in the organization. And you can have that as a woman as well, but in most cases, men are the ones that benefits from this ideal. This is a structural problem that stands in the way of creating an inclusive organization.

Others, like Henryk from Poland, pointed out that competency only takes you so far, as there is more to participation than access. When he started playing golf, just for fun, the clubhouse manager came over and said:

'next time you play just please make sure your socks are a bit higher like they're just got shorts and the socks are very low and just make it higher'. ... I wasn't expecting that even from like a Polish background you know this was completely normal for them for my colleagues you know the British they're like 'yeah of course yeah that's fine' because that's that's in most in most British clubs for me it was just unbelievable. I was very surprised. I know they're traditional clubs and this is something I've personally never liked and with the jeans example as well I mean looking at like the history of why jeans were not allowed on the golf courses ...the only reason is for golfers to be uh you know not to be mixed with the working class which wore jeans back in the day

As such leaders should take the organizational culture and structures into account in their quest to facilitate participatory self-efficacy.

A second way to build self-efficacy is through what Bandura calls vicarious experiences. Vicarious experiences involve seeing people who are relatable to oneself, succeed based on their efforts (Bandura, 1997). A central concept here in relation to leadership is the idea of leaders as role models and the use of mentoring (Shamir, 1991; Yan et al., 2022). This is pictured by Alise who uses herself as an example when she explains how leaders can increase participation through social inclusion in sport:

> Another way is, of course, to make sure that we have leaders or people in the leadership positions from different backgrounds, because especially from the discussions we had with the young people, it encourages them a lot. Then they hear the stories that the leaders or people in the positions, they come from different backgrounds, maybe different disabilities, disadvantages, and etc. Me, myself, I also usually share my story. I also came from a very small town. I mean, I grew up in the town which had 5,000 people. So it's a very, very small city in Lithuania. And then they come and say, okay, but you talk with thousands of people. You have these presentations with the huge crowds and etc. So this story also inspires for different inclusion aspects, let's say.

Leaders are therefore important role models, by speaking up themselves and thereby enhancing voice self-efficacy. For example, Henryk applauded the employment in some clubs of people who 'are actually quite forward looking and, you know, pushing the game forward.' He used an example from Scotland where one individual has done a lot make the club 'an extremely open facility, working with the community.' But behind the scenes, the organization stays intact 'with just a room of old golf club members. Old and rich and they can fire and hire whoever and no one has any control over what they do.' Although the examples presented show the importance of role models, a challenge may lie in the lack of role models from marginalized groups that speak up. For example, Yan et al. (2022) argue that a reason why women may voice their opinions less than men is because of an absence of female leaders who model speaking up. Because of this, women may experience less access to mastery experiences with speaking up, and thereby also miss out on the chance to develop voice self-efficacy (Wood & Karten, 1986). Wood and Karten (1986) argue that 'status cues lead people to have expectations about each other's behavior so that people who have characteristics (e.g., maleness) ordinarily associated with higher status roles in our society are assumed to be more competent' (p. 341). Therefore, specific mentoring programs may be of particular relevance when aiming to increase voice self-efficacy in sports. Lefebvre et al. (2020) argue that mentoring is effective in increasing knowledge and skills in both athletes and coaches. However, based on social cognitive theory (Bandura, 1997), it is pertinent to note that individuals from marginalized groups can observe individuals that are congruent with the groups they socially identify with, as this will help them perform specific elements of agentic behaviour such as speaking up and sharing their opinions (Yan et al., 2022). The importance of mentoring for facilitating confidence and efficacy in participatory practices is highlighted by Alise who explains that:

> Mentoring, that's a very first step. So we need this mentoring program to have concrete people who would be support at the beginning. And I think that's not only for inclusion aspect. I think this is in general for the youth aspect. There is the biggest mistake when they say, 'oh, we give a space, we give an opportunity, they can do whatever.' It doesn't work like that. You need to have a mentor who at least at the beginning helps. And then, of course, you can leave them do. But at least for the beginning, we need that.

The last way of increasing self-efficacy according to social cognitive theory, that is relevant to our context, is through social persuasion. Social persuasion is concerned with offering encouragement, specific feedback, and creating environments where you are not punished for trying (Bandura, 1997). These factors are all relatable to Veli Korkmaz et al.'s (2022) model of inclusive leadership. In this model, one of the dimensions, showing appreciation, entails recognizing efforts and contributions, directly relatable to Bandura's (1997) focus on positive encouragement. In relation to increasing participatory self-efficacy, this means acknowledging and appreciating inputs from marginalized groups and creating environments characterized by a growth mindset where effort and improvement are valued over performance and criticism (Yeager & Dweck, 2020). The importance of inclusive leadership for increasing speaking up is empirically supported by Younas et al. (2023). Their quantitative study finds that inclusive leadership, specifically through a focus on participation in decision-making processes, both directly and indirectly through the mechanism of empowerment, increases individuals' propensity to speak up.

To round off, our emphasis on self-efficacy as a tool to go from representation, or the availability of access, to participation for social inclusion relates to the key finding in Chapter 3 – on the necessity of dialogue between parties. As such, it bears on the literature on inclusive leadership, which underlines the importance of sharing decisions and appreciating inputs (Carmeli et al., 2009; Korkmaz et al., 2022). Our finding relevant to practice is summarized in Table 4.1. As the concepts involved in exploring participation bear some overlap, the initiatives for facilitating participation also contain overlapping issues.

Table 4.1 Practical perspectives on participation and social inclusion

	Understood as	Operationalized through	Facilitated by
Participation	The social range of participation	The involvement of diverse stakeholders on social inclusion issues	Denoting time for inclusion issues Sharing influence on relevant issues Leader competence and self-awareness Avoiding pseudo-participation, by fostering genuine power sharing
	Balancing formal and informal participation	Establishing a culture of voice	Stimulating cultural and organizational knowledge Stimulating psychological safety by being approachable, participative, and valuing upward communication of ideas and concerns Striving towards organizational values and structures that allow for disagreement and conflicting perspectives.
	The complexities of the decisions being addressed	Fostering competence and self-efficacy regarding participation	Emphatically connect with diverse stakeholders and applying cultural knowledge Fostering voice self-efficacy by • Creating safe arenas for individuals to get mastery experiences with participation • Making differences transparent and visible • Having relevant role models for voice

Concluding remarks

This chapter has been concerned with participation and has covered topics such as influence sharing, power and competence as factors pivotal to increase social inclusion through sport. Our findings point to the importance of not taking for granted that participation and influence sharing will take place if people are given a 'seat at the table.' Rather, for people to express and participate, they need to be asked, to be granted time to express their views and to feel that they are safe and competent to participate. As such, the potential for sport to influence social inclusion issues is conditioned and can be facilitated by leaders who pay attention to these issues and are genuinely interested in understanding and considering the views of marginalized groups.

A challenge lies in that leaders may be afraid to lose influence and power if they authentically share their influence. Yet, from a social justice perspective, this challenge needs to be grappled with by leaders to foster social inclusion through sport. The concepts of participation, power, influence and self-efficacy are all factors central to reach what Gidley et al. (2010a, 2010b) suggest as the most inclusive definition of social inclusion, empowerment. As such, we will now turn to the next chapter and explore what leaders can do to create social inclusion through the experience of meaningfulness in sport.

References

Argyris, C. (1976). Theories of action that inhibit individual learning. *American Psychologist*, *31*(9), 638. https://doi.org/10.1037/0003-066X.31.9.638

Bandura, A. (1997). *Self-efficacy: The exercise of control*. Macmillan.

Bandura, A. (2006). Toward a psychology of human agency. *Perspectives on Psychological Science*, *1*(2), 164–180. https://doi.org/10.1111/j.1745-6916.2006.00011.x

Carmeli, A., Sheaffer, Z., & Yitzack Halevi, M. (2009). Does participatory decision-making in top management teams enhance decision effectiveness and firm performance? *Personnel Review*, *38*(6), 696–714. https://doi.org/10.1108/00483480910992283

Dachler, H. P., & Wilpert, B. (1978). Conceptual dimensions and boundaries of participation in organizations: A critical evaluation. *Administrative Science Quarterly*, 1–39. https://doi.org/10.2307/2392432

Darnell, S. C., & Millington, R. (2018). Social justice, sport, and sociology: A position statement. *Quest*, *71*(2), 175–187. https://doi.org/10.1080/00336297.2018.1545681

Detert, J. R., & Burris, E. R. (2007). Leadership behavior and employee voice: Is the door really open?. *Academy of Management Journal*, *50*(4), 869–884. https://doi.org/10.5465/amj.2007.26279183

Edmondson, A. (1999). Psychological safety and learning behavior in work teams. *Administrative Science Quarterly*, *44*(2), 350–383. https://doi.org/10.2307/266699

Edmondson, A. C., & Bransby, D. P. (2023). Psychological safety comes of age: Observed themes in an established literature. *Annual Review of Organizational Psychology and Organizational Behavior*, *10*(1), 55–78. https://doi.org/10.1146/annurev-orgpsych-120920-055217

Foucault, M. (2013). *Archaeology of knowledge*. Routledge. https://doi.org/10.4324/9780203604168

Gallie, D. (2013). Direct participation and the quality of work. *Human Relations*, *66*(4), 453–473. https://doi.org/10.1177/0018726712473035

Gidley, J., Hampson, G., Wheeler, L., & Bereded-Samuel, E. (2010a). Social inclusion: Context, theory and practice. *The Australasian Journal of University-Community Engagement*, *5*(1), 6–36.

Gidley, J. M., Hampson, G. P., Wheeler, L., & Bereded-Samuel, E. (2010b). From access to success: An integrated approach to quality higher education informed by social inclusion theory and practice. *Higher Education Policy*, *23*, 123–147 https://doi.org/10.1057/hep.2009.24

Harris, K. & Adams, A. (2016). Power and discourse in the politics of evidence in sport for development. *Sport management review*, *19*(2), 97–106. https://doi.org/10.1016/j.smr.2015.05.001

Heller, F. (2003). Participation and power: A critical assessment. *Applied Psychology*, *52*(1), 144–163. https://doi.org/10.1111/1464-0597.00128

Heller, F. (2019). Influence at work: A 25-year program of research. In *Managing democratic organizations II* (pp. 415–446). Routledge.

Hoeber, L. (2007). Exploring the gaps between meanings and practices of gender equity in a sport organization. *Gender, Work and Organization*, *14*(3), 259–280. https://doi.org/10.1111/j.1468-0432.2007.00342.x

Kahn, W. A. (1990). Psychological conditions of personal engagement and disengagement at work. *Academy of management journal*, *33*(4), 692–724. https://doi.org/10.5465/256287

Khechen, M. (2013). Social justice: Concepts, principles, tools and challenges. *A publication of the United Nations economic and social Commission for West Asia; United Nations economic and social council*.

Kidd, B. (2008). A new social movement: Sport for development and peace. *Sport in society*, *11*(4), 370–380. https://doi.org/10.1080/17430430802019268

Knudsen, H., Busck, O., & Lind, J. (2011). Work environment quality: The role of workplace participation and democracy. *Work, Employment and Society*, *25*(3), 379–396. https://doi.org/10.1177/0950017011407966

Korkmaz, A. V., Van Engen, M. L., Knappert, L., & Schalk, R. (2022). About and beyond leading uniqueness and belongingness: A systematic review of inclusive leadership research. *Human Resource Management Review*, *32*(4), 100894. https://doi.org/10.1016/j.hrmr.2022.100894

Lange, S., Bolt, G., Vos, S., & Völker, B. (2024). Inclusion of the marginalized: The case of sport participation: A scoping review. *Journal of Global Sport Management*, 1–29. https://doi.org/10.1080/24704067.2024.2317121

Lefebvre, J. S., Bloom, G. A., & Loughead, T. M. (2020). A citation network analysis of career mentoring across disciplines: A roadmap for mentoring research in sport. *Psychology of Sport and Exercise*, *49*, https://doi.org/10.1016/j.psychsport.2020.101676

Liang, J., Farh, C. I., & Farh, J. L. (2012). Psychological antecedents of promotive and prohibitive voice: A two-wave examination. *Academy of Management journal*, *55*(1), 71–92. https://doi.org/10.5465/amj.2010.0176

Liu, W., Zhu, R., & Yang, Y. (2010). I warn you because I like you: Voice behavior, employee identifications, and transformational leadership. *The Leadership Quarterly*, *21*(1), 189–202. https://doi.org/10.1016/j.leaqua.2009.10.014

Liu, Y. D. (2009). Sport and social inclusion: Evidence from the performance of public leisure facilities. *Social Indicators Research*, *90*, 325–337. https://doi.org/10.1007/s11205-008-9261-4

Mutz, M., & Müller, J. (2021). Social stratification of leisure time sport and exercise activities: Comparison of ten popular sports activities. *Leisure Studies*, *40*(5), 597–611. https://doi.org/10.1080/02614367.2021.1916834

Nicholls, A. R., Polman, R. C. J., Levy, A. R., & Borkoles, E. (2010). The mediating role of coping: A cross-sectional analysis of the relationship between coping self-efficacy and coping effectiveness among athletes. *International Journal of Stress Management*, *17*(3), 181–192. https://doi.org/10.1037/a0020064

Piggott, L. V., Hovden, J., & Knoppers, A. (2024). Why organization studies should care more about gender exclusion and inclusion in sport organizations. In S. Clegg, M. Grothe-Hammer, & K. S. Velarde (eds.), *Sociological thinking in contemporary organizational scholarship* (pp. 201–226). Emerald.

Shamir, B. (1991). Meaning, self and motivation in organizations. *Organization studies*, *12*(3), 405–424. https://doi.org/10.1177/017084069101200304

Svendsen, M., Jønsson, T. S., & Unterrainer, C. (2016). Participative supervisory behavior and the importance of feeling safe and competent to voice. *Journal of Personnel Psychology*, *15*(1), 25–34. https://doi.org/10.1027/1866-5888/a000146

Tangirala, S., & Ramanujam, R. (2012). Ask and you shall hear (but not always): Examining the relationship between manager consultation and employee voice. *Personnel Psychology*, *65*(2), 251–282. https://doi.org/10.1111/j.1744-6570.2012.01248.x

Veiga, J. F. (1991). The frequency of self-limiting behavior in groups: A measure and an explanation. *Human Relations*, *44*(8), 877–895. https://doi.org/10.1177/001872679104400807

Vignesh, M. (2020). Decision making using Vroom-Yetton-Jago model with a practical application. *International Journal for Research in Applied Science and Engineering Technology*, *8*(10), 330–337. https://doi.org/10.22214/ijraset.2020.31876

Vroom, V. H., & Jago, A. G. (1974). Decision-making as a social process: Normative and descriptive models of leader behavior. *Decision Sciences*, *5*, 743–769. https://doi.org/10.1111/j.1540-5915.1974.tb00651.x

Vroom, V. H., & Jago, A. G. (1978). On the validity of the Vroom-Yetton model. *Journal of Applied Psychology*, *63*(2), 151–162. https://doi.org/10.1037/0021-9010.63.2.151

Wood, W., & Karten, S. J. (1986). Sex differences in interaction style as a product of perceived sex differences in competence. *Journal of Personality and Social Psychology*, *50*(2), 341.

Yan, T., Tangirala, S., Vadera, A. K., & Ekkirala, S. (2022). How employees learn to speak up from their leaders: Gender congruity effects in the development of voice self-efficacy. *Journal of Applied Psychology*, *107*(4), 650. https://doi.org/10.1037/apl0000892

Yeager, D. S., & Dweck, C. S. (2020). What can be learned from growth mindset controversies?. *American Psychologist*, *75*(9), 1269. https://doi.org/10.1037/amp0000794

Younas, A., Wang, D., Javed, B., & Haque, A. U. (2023). Inclusive leadership and voice behavior: The role of psychological empowerment. *The Journal of Social Psychology*, *163*(2), 174–190. https://doi.org/10.1080/00224545.2022.2026283

5 The role of leadership in stimulating empowerment

Introduction

The last dimension in Gidley et al.'s (2010a) model of social inclusion, is empowerment. While Chapter 4 concerned the processes that happen 'around the table', the current chapter explores what happens after people leave the table and interact with society. According to Gidley et al. (2010a), seeing social inclusion through the perspective of empowerment is the most integrative understanding of social inclusion and goes beyond the social justice perspective as it 'foregrounds the notion that all human beings (whether mainstream or marginalized) are multi-dimensional beings, who have needs and interests that go well beyond their role in the political economy of a nation' (p. 11). Moreover, Gidley et al. (2010b) affirm that seeing social inclusion through the lens of empowerment 'valorizes difference and diversity, pointing to collective individualism' (p. 5). Central to this understanding is the valuing of human potential and a shift from deficiency focus to human potential and strengths. The essence of empowerment is captured in the reflections made by Lydia, a leader from Greece working with social inclusion of immigrant and refugees through sport. She explains that:

> You need to consider who is to be included and who is to include, because I think inclusion in itself has a distinction between a superior that will include an inferior. It's the same thing with the migrants and refugees. They should be included in our European community. And so even discussing inclusion from these two different sides from a European person, and a migrant or a refugee, brings you two different definitions.

Lydia highlights at least three aspects relevant to understanding the importance of empowerment in a social inclusion context. First, social inclusion is related to the feeling of being inferior (or the opposite). Second, subjectivity; how social inclusion is understood is relative to the

DOI: 10.4324/9781003527848-5

This chapter has been made available under a CC-BY-NC-ND license.

individual's perception of the context. Third, she exemplifies the diversity of understandings of how social inclusion should be defined. Together, these reflections are all of importance to the understanding of the relationship between empowerment and social inclusion. Connecting these aspects to empowerment is, however, not straightforward, as empowerment is a contested construct. According to Drydyk (2017) 'it is nearly customary by now to begin a conceptual article on empowerment by lamenting how confused the concept has become over the last decade' (p.17). For example, empowerment can be understood as both a process and an end. As a process, it can relate to reversing powerlessness experienced by marginalized individuals. As an end, however, it is not only about giving people more choices and confidence to participate (as discussed in Chapter 4), but about giving individuals real opportunities to create a better life situation (Drydyk et al., 2023).

Thus, empowerment involves a socio-structural and a psychological element that is both central to the understanding of empowerment in relation to sport. Correspondingly, we will investigate what leaders in sport can do to stimulate social inclusion through the experience of psychological empowerment? To explore this question, the chapter will proceed as follows; in the next section, empowerment and its relation to social inclusion will be presented. Second, the concept of empowerment will be unpacked by using Spreitzer's (1995) model of empowerment to explore what leaders can do to increase social inclusion through empowerment in sport by fostering a) meaningfulness, b) self-determination, c) competence, and d) impact. Lastly, critical and practical reflections regarding psychological empowerment in sport will be discussed, together with some concluding remarks.

Empowerment and social inclusion in sport

In relation to sport, empowerment has been conceptualized in various ways. Lawson (2005) highlights three keys to understanding empowerment in sport. One key is the availability of resources, ranging from money to assistance networks. Thus, for a person or community to experience empowerment through sport, access is needed. This part of the empowerment concept is discussed in depth in Chapter 3. Another key to understanding empowerment in sport is through power and power sharing According to Lawson (2005), 'in order to know empowerment when you see it, you need to understand power distributions and authority relations, and you need to be able to determine how they change for the better as empowerment is practiced' (p. 147). This key to understanding empowerment is related to participation, as discussed in Chapter 4. These two understandings of empowerment can arguably be interpreted in accordance with the socio-structural understanding of empowerment (Spreitzer, 2008) that puts weight on power and how organizational, institutional, social, political, or cultural forces can create conditions that may or may not lead to empowerment (Liden & Arad, 1996). The third key to understanding the empowerment concept in relation to sport, according to Lawson (2005), rests on the foundation of collaboration and entails collaborative engagement, where participants manifest their needs and wants and how they will get access to them and represents a more psychological understanding of the empowerment concept.

In contrast to the predominant attention to the socio-structural aspects of empowerment (Drydyk, 2017), the psychological element of the concept has been somewhat overlooked in research on social inclusion and empowerment in sport. This lack of research on psychological empowerment is unfortunate, as it forms a cornerstone in the stimulation of organizational and community empowerment, which might be rectified by studies that 'examine and identify what are the psychologically empowering process and outcomes in the context of sport participation' (Lim & Dixon, 2017, p. 402). For example, Jakob from Austria said that one of the upsides of working with social inclusion was 'seeing how impactful a socially including time on the field/in the club can be for a young person, it is a great way to develop a person's personality in a positive way.' As such, empowerment can be viewed as establishing and facilitating meaningfulness for the individual and the collective, by inviting people's agentic engagement in activities on their own terms. Lawson's (2005) third key to understanding empowerment also stresses the importance of community and belonging, in the same vein that Gidley et al. (2010a) underline the importance of collective individualism to experience empowerment. On that note, we interpret Lawson's last key to understanding empowerment in line with the concept of psychological empowerment which underlines how the individual subjectively experiences their environment, rather than how it is objectively structured (Spreitzer, 2007). In this regard, Crisp (2020), who researched empowerment and community sport projects, underlines that many of 'the intended consequences of promoting empowerment can be measured through individuals' actions and self-regulation, and so in many respects it can be seen to detail a psychological change' (p. 224). Lydia gives an important example from practice of the importance of psychological empowerment and how participating in an activity is not enough to reach this ideal. When discussing the relationship between participation and empowerment, she explains that participation in sport can be both a vehicle and a hindrance for empowerment, and how she has experienced that some people want to 'prove that you are useless.' She gives an example of how participation in sport can negatively impact empowerment:

> I have Afghani boys, Syrian boys, Egyptian boys that play street soccer and then I take them to clubs in Greece and they have no idea of the regulations of a European soccer game. So I throw them in there and

yes, they can participate and I yell at them because they don't know what they're doing, and this is not empowerment. So participation needs to be very well controlled, designed, prepared, planned by the coach, the trainer, the person who is in charge.

Much empirical work on empowerment, however, has reduced the meaning of empowerment to Lawson's two first keys of empowerment, or what Drydyk (2013) refers to as power distribution or agency. This is unfortunate considering how being given power or choice over aspects of your life in such a way that does not, for example, have meaning for you, does not lead to the experience of empowerment (Spreitzer, 1995).

Accordingly, in this chapter we base our understanding of empowerment on the work of Spreitzer (1995, 2007, 2008), who sees empowerment as a motivational construct that involves the feeling of being able to shape one's own role and context. Spreitzer (1995) contends that psychological empowerment is built by experiencing meaning, self-determination, competence, and impact. To experience psychological empowerment, individuals should experience all four of these psychological states, and empowerment thus becomes a 'gestalt of the four dimensions' (Spreitzer, 2007, p. 8). This is important to keep in mind during the rest of the chapter, as there will obviously be some overlap between the dimensions and the factors that facilitate them. According to Spreitzer, empowerment should be understood as a continuous variable. This means that individuals are not categorized as empowered or not empowered, but rather as more or less empowered. In accordance with research on self-efficacy (Bandura, 2001), empowerment should be regarded as domain-specific (Spreitzer, 2008), partly because of the interpretative diversity in play. Thomas and Velthouse (1990), whose study preceded and influenced Spreitzer's analysis, highlight the need to view self-efficacy judgments as 'subjective interpretations (constructions) of reality, so that task assessments are also influenced by individual differences in interpretive processes' (p. 667). Thus, in a sport context, empowerment can vary depending on the sport, context or participant demographics (Lim & Dixon, 2017). One may feel empowered as an athlete, but not as an employee or the opposite. The remainder of the chapter will address this through Spreitzer's (1995) fourfold model for analysing empowerment: meaningfulness, competence, impact, and self-determination.

Meaningfulness

According to Spreitzer (1995), meaning involves the significance of goals and purpose, and how these are perceived according to one's own ideals or standards. As such, meaning refers to a fit between the requirements in a role, and the individuals' beliefs, values and behaviours. There are many important sources of meaning (Rosso et al., 2010). In a review by

Maneka (2023) social relationships are established as the most important source of meaning. Hence, in our discussion of meaning in relation to empowerment and social inclusion we focus on belonging. Stillman and Baumeister (2009) argue that belonging poses a primary mechanism for meaning making in individuals. They ground the importance of belonging in an evolutionary perspective and argue that 'humans get most of what they need to survive from their social group, rather than directly from the environment' (p. 250). Thus, they contend that social exclusion could 'threaten people at such a basic level that it would impair their sense of meaningful existence' (Stillman & Baumeister, 2009, p. 250). Stillman and Lambert (2013) highlight the importance of the subjective experience of belonging.

For example, it is possible to be part of a sports club with friendly people and still not feel that one belongs or is accepted. One of our informants, Stina from Finland, working with social inclusion of LGBTQ+ individuals through sport, underlined this when she explained that 'if there's still like even one person in a team who's not doing the inclusion, but is doing exclusion, then somebody can still feel excluded. So it sort of also takes everybody to welcome someone.' In his article discussing the concept of belonging in relation to community football for refugees Stone (2018) argues that belonging in sport is 'an embodied sense of control, comfort and security; the ease through which one can convey both socially constructed and self-conceived identities' (p. 174). Moreover, he contends that

> Belonging, or the absence thereof, is regarded as the interconnection of personal identity, group attachment and cultural background. These characteristics are by no means independent from one another but emerge at different times to greater or lesser degrees to create feelings of belonging within individuals. Thus, it is not a fixed state but an ideal towards which each and every one of us proceeds, some more successfully than others.
>
> (p. 175)

As such, belonging to a category is not an ontological fact, but something that is dynamically construed by individuals and groups (Tajfel & Turner, 1986). Fehsenfeld (2015) finds empirical support for the notion that belonging is pivotal for the social construction of meaning within sport programmes for the socially disadvantaged, as it contributes to shared values, norms, social cohesion, and reduces the risk of rejection and failure. The importance of belonging was highlighted as a cornerstone for social inclusion by many of our informants. For example, Henryk, a Polish leader working with social inclusion issues in golf, was asked why social inclusion was an important issue to him. He explained that:

I think the biggest thing or the first thing that comes to my mind would be the integration aspect, the common experiences and common background, especially common experiences across different people, nationalities, genders and all the other different categories (...) which later like helps with empathy and like connection, which then would have like social inclusion.

In the same vein, Zoe from Greece, who was working with social inclusion issues with immigrants and refugees, stated that the most important thing for social inclusion is 'the sense of belonging because these people need this sense, the sense of someone is caring. I think that's the most important thing.' Correspondingly, Craig, a leader from the UK working with social inclusion issues for people with physical and intellectual disabilities, explained that the most beneficial outcome of social inclusion is:

people feeling like they belong somewhere. They're part of a club. They're not isolated. It's not the sports development. Yeah, we want to help them be better at kicking a ball. Yes, we want to help them be better at learning to serve in tennis. That's not as important as people feeling like they belong to a club. They can interact not only with other people, but also community environments. They get to go to their local clubs.

In the same vein, the absence of a sense of belonging and the subjective factor in experiencing it is considered an important barrier to social inclusion. Stina explains that:

if you belong to a team but you don't feel included and you still do the sports
there, then (...) the situation should be changed somehow. So you should bring it up or change the team or something. Because in the long run, it's not good for you, even if you get the physical exercise. But being excluded for a long time makes people just sad.

Lydia gave a vivid explanation of why sport is so pivotal for the feeling of belonging by creating the experience of identity and meaning and label sport as a 'passport' for immigrants coming to Greece:

They belong because they speak the same language, even if they don't speak Greek, but they play very good soccer. Usually it's soccer they play. And they belong. And not only they have this sense of belonging, but what's more important, they have this sense of continuity that they've lost. Because they can take away your country, your home, your people. But usually, if you have another identity, which is very strong, and being an athlete is a very strong identity, they cannot take it away from you.

Interestingly, however, Craig explains that the experience of belonging may not limit itself to the individuals vulnerable to marginalization in the first place. It may also spread and have a positive effect of belonging for the people who are close to these individuals. For example, Craig elaborates on the unintended consequence of a social inclusion project, where respite sessions are provided for children with complex needs, so their parents are able to have some respite care. Craig explains that this allows children with complex needs to form a community and participate in sport. However, an unintended consequence of the initiative was how:

> all the parents of the different children start talking to each other and they start to support each other because they're all living through these challenges in the same way. Before, they had no one to share them with, but now they're in a community where they're all in the same position and they share, they talk, they laugh.

He concludes that 'what we do it for is that social element between child, family and the wider community,' underlining the importance of belonging for the people who are involved with people vulnerable to exclusion. Judit from Slovenia highlighted how and why the mechanism of belonging is of such high importance for people from marginalized groups, by referring to the difference between strong and weak ties in the social network of athletes participating in judo. According to Granovetter (1973), strong and weak ties can be understood as the amount of time, the intensity, the intimacy, and the services shared between two nodes in a social network. Dobbels et al. (2018) confirm that network structure is of relevance for the social inclusion projects in sport for disadvantaged people. Maness (2017) also specifies this finding and illustrates how the diversity of weak ties and access to weak ties with high social status, positively affects the frequency of leisure participation. Judit explained that individuals with intellectual disabilities often have the same strong ties (for example, family) as other participants. However, the weak ties, meaning the more loosely defined social networks, seem to be more vulnerable for people with intellectual disabilities and sport therefore has an even stronger meaning for them. She explains:

> I was working a lot with intellectual disability. They don't have so many weak ties. And that's why they are weaker in society. And that's why the sports club means so much to them because this is one way out of the family that is like a window to society, to let's say to a normal world.

The importance of the weak ties is thus not only that individuals vulnerable to exclusion get access to a larger network, but also that they get access to a network that knows and appreciates them on their own terms.

As such, our findings support experimental studies that suggest that feeling well liked, welcomed, and popular is linked to a higher belief that life has meaning (Stillman & Lambert, 2013) and that social exclusion leads to a decrease in meaning (Stillman & Baumeister, 2009).

Creating meaningfulness through the experience of belonging – the role of leadership

Having established the importance of belonging for social inclusion and meaningfulness a pertinent question becomes; what can leaders do to increase the part of the psychological empowerment concept related to meaningfulness? First, leaders need to be consistent when it comes to supporting the organizational efforts to be inclusive (Veli Korkmaz et al., 2022). Moreover, they need to communicate inclusiveness as a value and standard early in the process. To effectively communicate the importance of inclusion, this communication needs to be both formal at an organizational level, but also trickle down to the informal interpersonal communication in the organization (Wolfgruber et al., 2022). Judit illustrates the importance of strongly supporting the value of inclusion and the importance of communicating it clearly; both formally in specific meetings, but also informal by for example conversations with parents of new members of the sport club:

> I had about maybe five people that [stopped coming] to our club because they were not feeling well being around people with disability. But I learned that we don't need those people. I was glad that it turned out that way. But now, as I'm continuing with this way of working, more and more people are coming to the club that really respect this inclusive approach. And every time some parents call me, I always say we are inclusive. We have people with us with diverse abilities and we are working a little bit different, is that OK with you? And most of them are saying, yes, perfect.

Stina also highlights the leader role when it comes to communication. She explains that:

> I think inclusion, well, the initiative needs to come from leadership, and they need to be active on it. If you just think that you are including everybody, you say everybody's welcome, that's usually not enough. So that's why it's important to actually have a communication that involves who you want to include (…) There can be campaigns. You can do it on your website. Mention what you're doing for different groups and so on.

Second, to create a feeling of belonging, it is beneficial for leaders to focus on the inclusion of the close network or the strong ties of the participants who are at risk of exclusion (Dobbels et al., 2018). Judit describes that it is pivotal that parents of children with disabilities are allowed to gain positive experiences from their environment, as they have often encountered so many challenging experiences from society. Therefore, she claims that one of her most important tasks is to include people with disabilities *and* their parents in judo. She says that:

> For me, my work is to make this air around us welcoming all the time – it's the biggest work in an inclusive sports club, I think, that somebody has to do. But yeah, it's not science, it's just a social worker mother bug.

A third important leadership task is to act as an 'identity entrepreneur' and be aware of how individuals at risk of marginalization can belong to different groups, without losing the importance of their most salient social identity (Fladerer et al., 2021). An example of this was provided by Zoe who told a story of when she was working in Mytilene, a reception centre in Moria. Many of the refugees had been there for up to five years and their living conditions were awful. Once she was counting the points in a volleyball game, and she said the points in Farsi, Arabic, English, and Greek:

> At the beginning I had one person, when I was telling it [the score] in Greek, he came to my face and said, 'not in Greek'. And I was trying to make a joke. But I didn't stop saying it in all languages. He came to my face two, three times. And after this, I was telling it in Greek and I was smiling at him, but I was smiling at him not laughing with him. And he stopped doing this. So you see, I can understand that being five years in a campus with very bad situations of living. Yes, he will be angry. He wants to live to go somewhere else. But okay, I can understand you, but this is something that I respect, but you should respect too.

Through her quiet, yet powerful insistence on also acknowledging the Greek numbers, Zoe was able to convey the plethora of social identities that was at stake for the volleyball team, and the player that resisted the Greek counting. The above example also underlines the importance of belonging as a dynamic and subjective experience (Tajfel & Turner, 1986; Stone, 2018). However, competing social identities can be an important barrier to social inclusion. Lydia highlights how the discourse on social inclusion in sport is often characterized by a focus on assimilation, and that we often want to include people into our sport (i.e., volleyball), but the participants may have no interest in this and would rather play for example hockey. She explains:

> Inclusion for the native European is assimilation. Because if it is inclusion, it is inclusion with limits. *I* include *you*. It's like with homosexual people, that I respect them, but I wouldn't like my son to be gay. I like

refugees and I don't mind refugees, but I don't want them in my neighborhood. It's better if they are in their own neighborhoods. I would like them in my sports club, but not as a captain. I want the captain of the team to be Greek.

A fourth way to create social inclusion through a sense of belonging in sport is through easing the competitive aspect of sport. On the one hand, the rules, regulations and competitive aspect of sport may be the very thing that makes it so suitable for social inclusion, as these rules are the same regardless of the participant's background (Bailey, 2007). On the other hand, it may be that these same rules and competitiveness create social exclusion in sport (Spaaij et al., 2014). Hansen et al. (2003) suggest that competition may be the key variable in producing both positive and negative outcomes through sport, and they conclude that 'processes associated with positive youth development may limit the development of collaborative skills and expose youth to negative experiences that challenge their character' (p. 51). In the same way, Bortoletto and Porrovecchio (2018) conclude that 'there is an important gap between reality and utopia: the reality of competition and the cult of victory come to oppose the utopic values of integration, so it would be risky to say that sport allows easy integration' (p. 54). Their point is illustrated in practice by Craig who also discusses how competitiveness in sport can hamper the feeling of belonging. For example, he explains that if you look at 'five to 11-year-olds in schools, if you watched the way the playground works, if you're not good at football, socially, it's going to be difficult to make friends.' He elaborates this further:

> I think there's still some work to be done in removing the elitist attitude (…) from teachers, coaches down to participants. But generally, if done in a way that's for the right reasons at the right level, because elitism has a place at academic, elite, pro-professional standards, but for grassroots, community and schools, it needs to remain for engagement, health and well-being elements.

Lydia illustrates this point further and frankly states that, 'if you are in a competitive club, there is no room for such thing as social inclusion.' To reduce the negative aspects from competition-driven sports inherent in the funding and structure of the European Model of Sport (EMS), Anders from Denmark argues that we need to acknowledge the wider diversity of physical activities. He contends that:

> One must also be honest in saying that sports have an insanely large number of practices, especially in the competitive-oriented part, which are simply not relevant, and may even be excluding for children and young people who fundamentally just want to have fun. And if they do

want the competitive element, then I think we should talk about it in a way that focuses on them competing with themselves and approaching competitions as a journey, more than focusing on the result.

In line with this, Zoe explains that one of her strategies to increase belonging among individuals with immigrant background is to balance competitiveness with cooperation. She elaborates on a situation where they struggled with violence at the school she was teaching. Thus, she modified her games and focused on trust building and communication training, and through that, the students learned to help, follow, guide and care for each other. She explains that:

> It wasn't easy. But all this effort, I think that the students learned that they are all accepted, that they were all respected and they learn how to cooperate with others and for me it was very important, they learned to care for the others. At the end, I didn't have any problem with the kids.

The last leadership behaviour that our informants put forth as pivotal to create a sense of belonging through social inclusion efforts is role modelling. As argued by Shore and Chung (2022), leaders have pivotal role in signalling how people are allowed to belong to the organization, while at the same time retaining their uniqueness. According to Emma from the UK, 'the development of people into leaders for their community has been very rewarding especially those who doubted they had the skills or confidence to become a leader.' Similarly, Mor Barak et al. (2022) argue that decoupling, meaning the failure to 'walk the talk' on inclusion issues, may harm the feeling of belonging to the organization. Zoe paints an interesting picture of the importance of role modeling when she discusses what she believes is the most important thing leaders can do to create inclusion through belonging: 'When I train people and my students, and physical education teachers, I always say that everything begins with us and ends with us. So if we try to make inclusion and we are not inclusive persons, it will not work.' In practice, Zoe believes this boils down to the leaders' self-awareness. She explains that:

> You can always be aware of your stereotype. So you need to use a language without criticism, without stereotypes, because you cannot say, 'OK, this is a game that is inclusive for both girls and boys,' and somehow say something that is stereotyping for girls, for example.

The reflection of Zoe sits well with previous studies which confirm the importance of adult role models and how the trust developed between coaches and participants is pivotal for the success of sport intervention programmes (Crisp, 2020). Lydia elaborates this further:

> We always talk about underprivileged groups, whether it is mental illness, whether it is disabilities, whether it is migrants, refugees, girls. I think inclusion always goes with an underprivileged group or vulnerable group, which I hate because I believe that no group is vulnerable. The conditions we create are vulnerable. But if you do not create a safe place, and people do not trust who you are, why you're doing what you're doing, how you will do it, what your interest is, it will never reach the goal.

Lydia therefore advocates the importance of trust and safety for empowerment. This is also highlighted as pivotal by Lim and Dixon (2017) who underline the relationship between safety, belonging and the development of competence, knowledge, and skills: 'an empowering process can occur when a program provides participants with a safe space and an experience that they can increase perceived control and competence, yield knowledge and skills, and allow one to engage in collective activities' (p. 403) To elaborate this further, we will now dive deeper into the competence element of the empowerment construct.

Competence

The second part of the empowerment construct is related to competence or self-efficacy (Spreitzer, 1995). While in the previous chapter we argued that enabling self-efficacy among stakeholders was pivotal for leaders to enhance real participation, it is equally important to make the changes which come from this participatory process evolve and last. According to Spreitzer (1995), competence is 'an individual's belief in his or her capability for perform activities with skill' (p. 1443). In relation to social inclusion, this can be seen as connected to the development of life skills. Life skills can be defined as: 'those skills that enable individuals to succeed in the different environments in which they live, such as school, home and in their neighborhoods' (Danish et al., 2004, p. 40). According to Turnnidge et al. (2014), life skills can be understood as cognitive skills (for example, developing cognitive flexibility or creativity), emotional skills (e.g., managing social anxiety or depressive symptoms) and social skills (such as cooperation and teamwork). Often, sport is considered a prime site for developing these skills (Ronkainen et al., 2020). Working with immigrants, Enzo from Italy told a story about how this could go both ways. Some participants take part in social inclusion programmes and then leave, never to be seen again. One of the participants, for example, began playing football and went on to do it for a living in Italy. The promise of this move, however, was shut down as the club went bankrupt and lost all of his personal documents. Although Enzo tried to help him out, the government would not grant him refugee status, which made him so disheartened that he gave up and moved back to Africa. Contrastingly, Enzo also told a story about a person who quickly expressed an interest in administration and leadership and went on to become a major community philanthropist in his home country.

A concept related to life skills and development thereof is life skills transfer. According to a review by Pierce et al. (2016), life skills transfer refers to

> the ongoing process by which an individual further develops or learns and internalizes a personal asset (i.e., psychosocial skill, knowledge, disposition, identity construction, or transformation) in sport and then experiences personal change through the application of the asset in one or more life domains beyond the context where it was originally learned.
>
> (p. 194)

Accordingly, sport is also related to psycho-social development, and positive identity as highlighted by Pierce et al. (2016). Henryk explains that personal traits such as integrity are developed through the premises on which golf is based in addition to mental health benefits, stating that what is developed through golf is 'definitely like honesty and integrity because of how golf is played (…) that lack of direct competition in golf (…) we don't play against someone directly.' However, as the literature on life skills also notes, the development of life skills or competence through sport often happens both implicitly and explicitly and typically revolves around emotional, cognitive, personal, or physical skills (Pierce et al., 2016; Holt et al., 2017; Camiré et al., 2022). This complexity is described by Zoe when she tells us what the refugees thought about the benefits of a social inclusion project in a reception area she was part of:

> We kept them occupied in a funny way and creative way because they were in reception areas and in accommodation centers. So we didn't have a lot of things to do during the day, the daily life. Physical activity helped them reduce stress, deal with negative thoughts, because a lot of people commit suicide or try to suicide when they are in these centers. They improved their sleep. That was very important for them. They made new friends.

Lydia even considered the social life skills and the transference thereof as definitional for her understanding of social inclusion. She explains that:

I can include you in my volleyball club. But if I include you through my volleyball club into the Greek community, then I have achieved a higher goal. Because to include you in a small local volleyball club is one thing. But if through this volleyball club, I open up your network to other clubs in Greece and to other volleyball players in Greece. And then they open their homes and then they become your friends and not only your teammates. Then I have included you in the Greek community through a sports club.

Achieving competence through life skills – the role of leadership

According to a recent review by Harmsel-Nieuwenhuis et al. (2022), many factors may influence the development and transfer of life skills. Specifically, they identified the characteristics of the individual, the design and staff working with the programmes, the inherent demands of sport, the safety of the environment, and social cohesion as pivotal for the development and transfer of life skills. Importantly, Crisp (2020) identified the importance of leadership in the empowerment process. Specifically, he found that:

> the success of their projects was primarily due to building relationships and identifying leaders, outlining examples of good practice. These include an emphasis on consultation, flexibility, and allowing the young people to be given choice and incremental levels of responsibility. It is worth noting that the coaches emphasised the fact that they had character development (pro-social behaviours) embedded as part of their programme outcomes and expected their interactions to drive this instead of sport in and of itself.
>
> (p. 232)

As such, many of the factors influencing the development and transferability of life skills are related to the socio-psychological and cultural factors that may foster belonging, as discussed in the previous section, as much as 'skills' in the form of functional capacities. According to Camiré et al. (2022) important specific life skills for youth in particular, associated with sport are physical (such as healthy living), personal (developing self-esteem) and social (engagement in society). Ronkainen et al. (2020) expand this argument by claiming that life skills in reality is also about existential learning, that is, how people 'are attuned to the world, find meaning and value in life, and make life choices' (p. 219) in relation to others. In that context, Ronkainen et al. (2020) also criticize the lack of specificity when it comes to explaining how these transfer processes work and why it is not always useful to subscribe 'to the economic and social cohesion agendas implicit in life skills' (p. 221). To develop these skills beyond a socio-economic paradigm, Nicolai from Denmark underlines the importance of meeting participants where they are and engaging in their challenges. He gives an example of a project that works specifically with this among young gamers:

> We want movement, we want physical togetherness, but the reality is that young people play, and if we want to reach them where they are, we need to be part of that. Local associations in Denmark and the rest of Europe, as part of their sports association, also have an eSports department, where young people come and meet them, but where they can also be drawn into the community within the association and into the health-promoting activities they have.

Nicolai also highlights the importance of cooperation, when discussing the development of life skills. He describes a project directed at schools that aim to include refugees:

> There are schools in Poland, Denmark, and Spain, as well as schools in Ukraine, that are brought together and engage in activities across these countries. This provides both social and cultural learning, and of course, it also fosters understanding and ownership among these children.

Although the development of life skills is often perceived as an implicit outcome of participation in sport (Holt et al., 2017), our informants also underlined the importance of programmes with empowerment and development of life skills as an explicit focus. Our Lithuanian informant, Alise, described an empowerment project for women that was targeted at fostering empowerment of women to become leaders in sport organizations with a focus on nurturing leader identity, offering mentoring, concrete leadership skills and so forth. Alise also reflected on the importance of wanting to make change if you are selected as a leader, and how you will go forward to change your environment. This is closely tied to the experience of making an impact, which we will explore further in the next section.

Impact

The third factor of Spreitzer's understanding of empowerment is impact. Spreitzer (1995) contends that impact is the degree to which an individual can influence strategic, administrative or operating outcomes (p. 1444). In other words, people must believe that their behaviour will influence what happens around them to feel empowered. Impact is also referred to as the opposite of learned helplessness (Seligman, 2002). Understood in a social inclusion context, impact is thus whether a person believes she or he can significantly affect, make a difference to, or influence this context. Importantly, impact differs from concepts such as locus of control, as, contrary to locus of control, impact is constantly shaped by the environment and is hence not a personality trait that can be generalized across situations (Spreitzer, 1995). The potential to have real impact gives people a reason to take the risk to accomplish something and is therefore closely connected to the concept of positive deviance (Spreitzer & Doneson, 2005). Grant et al. (2007) introduce the term perceived impact and refer to this as the subjective awareness of how one's actions affect one's outcomes. In their measure of perceived impact, Grant et al. (2007) highlight the possibility of making a positive impact, to feel capable of making a change, to feel focused on improving, and the positive intention of trying to make something better. Grant et al. (2007) find that contact and feedback from beneficiaries is positively linked to the perception of making an impact. As such, impact is also connected to having a sense of purpose and trying to change something for the better (Rosso et al., 2010).

Impact can manifest itself in different ways in practice. Importantly, however, making an impact needs to be related to meaning to foster empowerment. The importance of meaning something to someone through sport is acknowledged by Van der Veken et al. (2020). The respondents in their study highlighted how getting responsibility, even a small one, gave the participants a sense of purpose, which in turn was one of the most important outcomes of their sport for development programme. They argue that many socially excluded people feel unworthy as they only receive and are not able to give something to others. However, sport can create arenas where this may be possible for these individuals (Van der Veken et al., 2020). Wilson (2000) claims that an important arena of making a positive impact in sport is through volunteering, that is, 'any activity in which time is given freely to benefit another person, group, or organization' (p. 215). Individuals at risk of exclusion are often underrepresented as a group in volunteering programmes and positions in sport. This is not surprising, considering that 'education, income and social networks are considered to be the most consistent predictors of volunteering' (Vertonghen et al., 2017, p. 181). Vertonghen et al. (2017) find in their study of a volunteering programme for underprivileged youths that one of the key factors contributing to social inclusion was the participants' experience of making a meaningful impact in society and their own neighbourhood. Alexandra from Norway underlines that volunteering is not only an important source of impact for oneself, but it is also empowering to see others making an impact. Alexandra explains that 'all children have the right to see that their parents are resources in the local community. And sports can contribute to this.'

She further argues that both school and local politics can accomplish this, but that 'it doesn't reach as many, but sports reach almost everyone, right?'

However, volunteering and parental volunteering through sport is not necessarily an unproblematic route to social inclusion. Legg and Karner (2021) find, in line with Alexandra's reflections, that volunteering may be an important route to empowerment through sport. However, their study also elucidates that sport volunteering is often a political process that is dependent on good social networks, rather than skills in the activity per se. Hence, as individuals at risk of exclusion may not have this network, the barriers to volunteering are larger. Whittaker and Holland-Smith (2016), investigate volunteering in relation to parental volunteering and find that the same exclusionary mechanisms are present here as well. The authors label this the 'dark side' of social capital and argue that the over-reliance of networks on parental volunteering may actually reinforce social exclusion mechanisms. This finding sits well with the reflections of Alexandra who describes how individuals and parents from marginalized groups may have trouble being recruited as volunteers out of a misunderstood form of kindness. Alexandra explains that:

> I know that there are native Norwegians (...) who don't know either Muslims or poor people, who refrain from asking because they don't want to add an extra burden. I have conducted research on parents who have come to Norway as refugees, and their first encounter is with kindergarten and how they experience never being asked to contribute as a form of exclusion.

This exemplifies Whittaker and Holland-Smith's (2016) dark side of volunteering and Alexandra concludes that:

> What the parents say is that they feel excluded. No one talks to them, and no one asks if they can bake buns. So it's not simple. But if we don't expand our conversations, if we don't open up to other perspectives, we will never be able to have those kinds of conversations. It will mean that we continue to reproduce exclusionary practices with the best of intentions.

The reflections of our informants underscored the importance of volunteering for making an impact. However, making an impact is not only about being something for others, it's also about achieving something for yourself. Dalsmo et al. (2021) find in their qualitative study of young Tanzanian women that the belief in one's own ability to achieve a personally significant outcome is a key factor to empowerment. This is also exemplified by Lydia who explains the importance of achievement, but also the inherent paradox leaders must face when working with these matters:

> A third element that we also see in schools when we're talking about inclusive education, but it's the same in sports, is opportunity to achieve something (...) if you do not have (...) opportunities, equal opportunities to achieve something, then again, we're not talking about full inclusion if it is only the natives. We cannot combine it. What leaders can do is provide both. Because if they do not provide both, then we become discriminatory.

Lydia also tells a story about two kids she was teaching in school with tremendous talent for sport:

> They were so above average that they needed something more that I could not provide them because I was doing physical education. I ended up having them as my assistants. We planned together. We break groups. They worked with their teammates and their classmates trying to help them. become more fit and more active and they found their role but as participants they were so good that they could not be part of it so it would be very unrealistic to say that we delete competitive sports because there's some charismatic people out there that they're meant to be in competitive sports.

Impact: the role of leadership

In order to give people an opportunity to perceive they have impact, it is pivotal that leaders are able to put themselves in the shoes of those they are working to include. Lydia gives an example involving a Coca-Cola ad which she often uses when giving talks about inclusion. In the commercial, someone is in the desert, almost dead from exhaustion, but then drinks Coca-Cola and gets refreshed and starts running again. However, it turned out this ad did not resonate with many refugees, as they read from the right to the left, so it looks like someone is almost dying if they drink Coca-Cola. Lydia explains that just like in the advertisement:

> We read the world differently from left to right. And we interpret things our own way. But there is a whole population out there that reads the world, not only differently, but in a completely opposite way. It's like we read inclusion from left to right or from right to left.

Another factor that can lead to a perception of impact is to tailor the competitive aspect of sport to the needs of the individual, to give them an opportunity to experience achievement. In their quest to find ways to compete in judo with a disability, Judit explains that:

> a window we found in judo is kata. In kata competitions, you don't compete with fighting, but with showing techniques. And it's very developing and very opening right now for people with disability and for those who don't want to compete in this traditional way, you know.

Lastly, it is important to be aware of how the different accessibility to networks may influence how leaders are recruited in the first place. In relation to the findings of Legg and Karner (2021), being appointed to leadership positions in volunteering may be related to who you know, more than what you know. Accordingly, and in relation to the findings in Chapter 3, leaders need to be aware of who is allowed a seat at the table. Additionally, Legg and Karner (2021) underscore the importance of inclusion as an embedded value of the organization, and that leaders need to play a part in the process of 'trickling down' these values, so that they also reach volunteers. These findings highlight the importance of Veli Korkmaz et al.'s (2022) inclusive leadership behaviour of supporting organizational efforts through championing and translating organizational values of inclusion into explicit behaviours.

Self-determination

The last factor in Spreitzer's (1995) model of empowerment is self-determination. Spreitzer (1995) contends that self-determination 'is an individual's sense of having choice in initiating and regulating actions' (p. 1443). According to Ryan and Deci (2000), the concept of self-determination is closely tied to the concept of autonomy. They argue that autonomy is not simply about the ability to choose between different options, but to engage in behaviour that is in correspondence with oneself. Autonomy is thus connected to, yet different from, participation in that:

> the concept of autonomy is a theoretical rather than empirical one, though it has clear empirical consequences. Autonomy connotes an inner endorsement of one's actions, the sense that they emanate from oneself and are one's own. Autonomous action is thus chosen, but we use the term choice not as a cognitive concept, referring to decisions among behavioral options (...), but rather as an organismic concept anchored in the sense of a fuller, more integrated functioning. The more autonomous the behavior, the more it is endorsed by the whole self and is experienced as action for which one is responsible.
>
> (Deci & Ryan, 1987, p. 2025)

To illustrate this point, Deci and Ryan (1987) give an example of an individual who is desperately seeking approval or avoiding guilt. They argue that, although this person may have choices of which behaviour to engage in, they are not autonomous because they are controlled by external factors that contribute to guilt, shame or lack of approval. Hence, when individuals are experiencing autonomy, they see themselves as the source of their behaviours, they can select which outcomes are important to them, and crucially, they can choose how they will go about trying to achieve them (Ryan & Deci, 2000). As such, one may question whether true autonomy, in an organismic perspective as proposed by Ryan and Deci (2000), is a utopic endeavour as there will always and inevitably be some external factors influencing the individual. However, autonomy should also be understood as a continuous variable, and an individual may thus experience autonomy to a smaller or larger extent (Deci & Ryan, 2008). Empirical findings support the importance of autonomy for the positive effect of sport on social inclusion. For example, Farello et al.'s (2019) study of a social inclusion programme for female youth refugees through sport endorses the importance of autonomy and choice for the experience of empowerment. The importance of autonomy and self-determination for social inclusion is underlined by Sabine from France. When asked about what she thinks is the most important outcome of social inclusion through sport, she affirms that

> the most important outcome would be to give people the opportunity to be where they are, where they want. But at the end of the day, I really think, yeah, it's about giving a chance for everyone to have their own journey in the context of sport.

The understanding of autonomy as a continuous variable is underlined by Lydia when she explains the dilemmas about her work with unaccompanied minors in Europe. She explains that:

> I have seen 16 year-olds with the mind of a 50-year-old. They have seen, experienced and been through things that we cannot even imagine and whether or not we Europeans wanted, these are not children. A 16-year-old unaccompanied minor is not a child. Yet, working for a state protection system, I need to take the decision for this child and tell him or her that you're going to live in a shelter. You're going to have a very strict curfew, like the curfew that I imposed to my son when he was 16 years old. When this kid came all the way from his country walking.

Lydia's take on this dilemma is to sit down with the individuals in question and reason and explain, and through that try to create a degree of ownership for the solution for them. She concludes that, 'we cannot make decisions for other people without them.' In a similar way, Roberto, a leader working with football for immigrants in Italy, underlines the importance of allowing people to experience that they are the source of their own action. Hence, it was the interest of the immigrants that led to their specific community project being about football. He described how they got to know a group of 20 or so guys coming from mostly Sub-Saharan Africa. When elaborating on the process of how this project became reality, he explained that:

> We tried to keep a strong connection with this group and to keep them involved and to let them take a decision and an idea of a project in what to do in the topic of inclusion. And since most of them were connected with football on many levels, their favorite game, also some of them coming to Italy with (…) the totally unrealistic illusion, to become a star in the sport and start playing in that field. So football was always there at some level. We decided to try to form a team and play a championship. It became a part of our local regular activity after the end of our international program just to keep these guys involved in the association and help them do something on their own, do something about what they love (…) what they want to do. Because some leaders stand in the way, whilst others help people become more of what they want to be themselves.

Roberto's quote also illustrates the fundamental part of leadership in relation to autonomy. This is something we will delve deeper into in the next section.

Leadership and self-determination

Lydia's work with unaccompanied minors in Europe highlights the necessity of involving individuals in decision-making processes to ensure their inclusion and respect their autonomy. This accords with Veli Korkmaz et al.'s (2022) focus on participative decision-making for fostering inclusion and for catering to the individuals' need to feel unique (Shore et al., 2011). Craig also acknowledges the importance of choice and attributes much of the success of his inclusionary efforts to the fact that they are striving to make it invitational and that the participants should be allowed to decide how they will go about achieving their goals. He explains that if participants want to try to do things differently:

> we shout about that and go 'oh look at this great idea let's all try and do it that way and allow people to explore.' One of the things that my coaches do as a leader, we say to all participants where we can that everything we do is invitational. So in our sessions there's not a coach

going 'right you must run to the cone'. So it allows individuals to choose on their journey of what they're doing.

Craig also argues that making activities invitational is both more ethical, but also that you get better responses from the participants. When he trains coaches to work with children with complex needs he explains to them:

> When you're at home with your partner (...) if they say to you, 'go and wash up,' what do you think? Well, 'don't tell me what to do.' But if you say, 'would you mind doing the washing up because I'm going to cook,' you get a much better response. And I try and use that example to what you can do with people in societies. You can do this or you can do that. Not 'this is what we're doing and you just have to get on with it.' So it's about allowing choice and making it invitational.

Yet Roberto also underlines that there may be instances where you grant autonomy and instances where you need to be more autocratic to pull the group forward. Moreover, he underlines the importance of perspective taking, by putting yourself on the same level as the participants. He explains that:

> I think that the first step in taking leadership the way that can facilitate other leaders to emerge is get rid of judgment, get rid of expectation (...) learn to put themselves on the same level of the participants and knowing that there's a distance between a leader and participants, but it's not the same distance every moment. You have to understand that there's a moment if you are totally a peer and you stay in the group, and there's a moment if you stand a little up and drag the whole group. Because doing just one of the things wouldn't be right. Just being at the same level doesn't make you a leader. Just standing out doesn't make you the leader that effectively helps the team grow.

Judit also underlines the importance of leaders giving individuals and parents from marginalized groups choice to explore and take part in meaningful activities in line with their own identity. However, she also illustrates how this choice is also pivotal for those who play an important part in marginalized individuals' life (i.e., parents). As such, it is not always given which group individuals wish to belong to, and leaders need to pay attention to this. Judit tells the story of 'Tina,' a girl with mild intellectual disability:

> After three years training with the mainstream group she said that, next year, I don't want to be in this group anymore. I want to be with my group. And I was shocked because of her expression, you know, because I was trying so hard for her to be in the middle of the, you

know, judo club and supporting her together with her parents. But then those were her words. I want to be with my people. And it was the first time that I was really starting to think, what are we actually doing by pushing them among us?

In the aftermath of this incident, Judit reflected a lot, and concluded that:

> I think that we need to listen to them much, much, much more than we do. And they don't bother being with their people. And they feel better maybe, you know. And it depends on us, our parents, how we push them and where we put them. So that's why I think it's so much important (...) to have choice, to have, you know, so they can choose. where they want to be, how long they want to be, and they're welcome and respected wherever, however they choose.

What Judit also shows is that formal structures, in this example mixed or exclusive groups, may not always be the most important thing to foster autonomy and sense of belonging for individuals at risk of marginalization. Rather, the important thing for 'Tina,' was that she was listened to and respected for her opinion on where she wanted to belong. This type of choice is also important for the people who are connected to the participants. Judit explains that:

> One kind of parents don't want to mix with a mainstream because in mainstream there are so many opportunities where they can be bullied or having a bad experience. So they like to be, you know, among them, among ours. So somehow separated because of feeling more or welcome or even safe. But then there are other kinds of parents who have children with disabilities, especially intellectual, who want to push and want to open worlds for their kids to have as much experience as possible and to live ... in the brackets [as] normal as possible but they somehow sacrifice their peace for the knowledge, for the experience that their children would get.

As can be seen from the reflections provided by the leaders in our study, autonomy or self-determination is more than simply being given the discretion of choice. It involves being given an authentic opportunity to create and choose a way of life that is in accordance with their own values, competence and idiosyncratic attributes. This authenticity and level of connection is summed up by Enzo who explains that the main job of leaders working with social inclusion in sport is to:

> try to connect always with people at some level. You can be the manager, you can be the trainer, you can be the social worker, but at the

moment you always have to look in the eyes of those who are in your project at any level. And this is something that actually is very heartfelt in the whole field of sport in our area. It's not about what you learn and the skill you bring. It's always about the capability to connect with the people when they need to

To round off the discussion of empowerment, social inclusion and leadership, the main findings of this chapter are presented in Table 5.1. It depicts the different leadership behaviours associated with the different dimensions of the empowerment constructs, but it is important to keep in mind the interrelatedness between the dimensions and how that also translates to the leadership behaviours associated with them.

Concluding remarks

In this chapter, we have looked at how sport can increase social inclusion through psychological empowerment, by stimulating meaningfulness, competence, impact and self-determination. As illustrated by many of our informants, however, these factors don't work in isolation and, in order to stimulate empowerment, leaders need to keep all these factors in mind. Considering our definition of social inclusion in Chapter 1, empowerment with regards to social inclusion issues, however, implies that leadership enables someone to feel that she can shape and define her role regarding her standing and worth in society, to create a feeling of belonging and of having a valued social identity.

The focus on psychological empowerment does not deny the structural constraints imposed on individuals vulnerable to social inclusion, as addressed in Chapter 3 and partially in Chapter 4. Critiques of psychological empowerment assert that it can function as a neo-liberal assimilation mechanism focusing on fixing individuals with deficiencies, so they become 'like the others' and making the individual themselves responsible for their growth, thriving and ability to be included, despite the structures that reinforce exclusionary mechanisms. Hence, empowerment needs to be understood within a critical perspective, aiming for agentic individuals, who are celebrated for their differences and become stimulated to use their strengths to alter their environment (Gidley et al., 2010b).

Accordingly, when sport leaders work with social inclusion and empowerment, they not only arrange for ballplayers; they help to convert a cluster of personal histories, identities, and statuses into a new stage through the world of sport. Individuals at risk of exclusion are not just that – they are complex human beings, for whom future sport leaders can be an inclusive or an exclusionary factor, regardless of sport because of the prominence of the social aspects involved.

Table 5.1 Practical perspectives on empowerment and social inclusion

	Defined as	Operationalized through	Facilitated by
Empowerment	Meaningfulness	Belonging	Internal and external communication of inclusive values Including the close network of individuals vulnerable to exclusion Navigating individuals' different and often competing social identities Balancing the competitive aspect of sport Role modelling and awareness of own stereotypes
	Competence	Life skills/life skills transfer	Meeting people where they are and where they have interest Having explicit focus on life skills (without the socio-economic factors frontline) Fostering learning through cooperation
	Impact	Volunteering and making a positive change	Asking people beyond the immediate network and being attentive to 'who is not at the table' (see also Chapter 3) Giving flexible opportunities for achieving through sport Perspective taking
	Self-determination	Autonomy	Allowing individuals their own journey in sport Facilitating bottom-up processes from the very start when initiating inclusive sport activities (also see Chapter 4) Dear to openly explore peoples' preferences for activities and belonging Value and facilitating human connection

References

Bailey, R. (2007). Youth sport and social inclusion. In N. L. Holt (ed.), *Positive youth development through sport* (pp. 99–110). Routledge.

Bandura, A. (2001). Social cognitive theory: An agentic perspective. *Annual Review of Psychology*, *52*, 1–26. https://doi.org/10.1146/annurev.psych.52.1.1

Bortoletto, N., & Porrovecchio, A. (2018). Social inclusion through sports: Comparing national policies on immigration and integration in Italy and France. *Society Register*, *3*(2), 42–55. https://doi.org/10.14746/sr.2018.2.1.03

Camiré, M., Newman, T. J., Bean, C., & Strachan, L. (2022). Reimagining positive youth development and life skills in sport through a social justice lens. *Journal of Applied Sport Psychology*, *34*(6), 1058–1076. https://doi.org/10.1080/10413200.2021.1958954

Crisp, P. (2020). Leadership, empowerment and coaching: How community sport coaches in the UK can effect behavioural change in disadvantaged youth through incrementally given roles of responsibility. *International Journal of Sport Policy and Politics*, *12*(2), 221–236. https://doi.org/10.1080/19406940.2020.1725095

Dalsmo, I. E., Haraldstad, K., Johannessen, B., Hovland, O. J., Chiduo, M. G., & Fegran, L. (2021). 'Now I feel that I can achieve something': Young Tanzanian women's experiences of empowerment by participating in health promotion campaigns. *International Journal of Environmental Research and Public Health*, *18*(16), 8747. https://doi.org/10.3390/ijerph18168747

Danish, S., Forneris, T., Hodge, K., & Heke, I. (2004). Enhancing youth development through sport. *World Leisure Journal*, *46*(1), 38–49. https://doi.org/10.1080/04419057.2004.9674365

Deci, E. L., & Ryan, R. M. (1987). The support of autonomy and the control of behavior. *Journal of Personality and Social Psychology*, *53*(6), 1024–1037. https://doi.org/10.1037/0022-3514.53.6.1024

Deci, E. L., & Ryan, R. M. (2008). Self-determination theory: A macrotheory of human motivation, development, and health. *Canadian Psychology/Psychologie canadienne*, *49*(3), 182–185. https://doi.org/10.1037/a0012801

Dobbels, L., Voets, J., Marlier, M., De Waegeneer, E., & Willem, A. (2018). Why network structure and coordination matter: A social network analysis of sport for disadvantaged people. *International Review for the Sociology of Sport*, *53*(5), 572–593. https://doi.org/10.1177/1012690216666273

Drydyk, J. (2013). Empowerment, agency, and power. *Journal of Global Ethics*, *9*(3), 249–262. https://doi.org/10.1080/17449626.2013.818374

Drydyk, J. (2017). Empowerment, agency, and power. In E. Palmer (ed.), *Gender justice and development: Vulnerability and empowerment* (pp. 17–30). Routledge.

Drydyk, J., Velasco, D., & O'Neill, K. (2023) Empowerment and poverty. In *The Routledge handbook of philosophy and poverty* (pp. 341–356). Routledge.

Farello, A., Blom, L., Mulvihill, T., & Erickson, J. (2019). Understanding female youth refugees' experiences in sport and physical education through the self-determination theory. *Journal of Sport for Development*, 7(13), 55–72.

Fehsenfeld, M. (2015). Inclusion of outsiders through sport. *Physical Culture and Sport. Studies and Research*, 65(1), 31–40. https://doi.org/10.1515/pcssr-2015-0009

Fladerer, M., Steffens, N. K., & Haslam, A. S. (2021). Bridging gaps in organizations: Leaders as entrepreneurs of identity. In Z. Jaser (ed.), *The connecting leader: Serving concurrently as a leader and a follower* (pp. 67–99). IAP.

Gidley, J., Hampson, G., Wheeler, L., & Bereded-Samuel, E. (2010a). Social inclusion: Context, theory and practice. *The Australasian Journal of University-Community Engagement*, 5(1), 6–36.

Gidley, J. M., Hampson, G. P., Wheeler, L., & Bereded-Samuel, E. (2010b). From access to success: An integrated approach to quality higher education informed by social inclusion theory and practice. *Higher Education Policy*, 23, 123–147 https://doi.org/10.1057/hep.2009.24

Granovetter, M. S. (1973). The strength of weak ties. *American Journal of Sociology*, 78(6), 1360–1380. https://doi.org/10.1086/225469

Grant, A. M., Campbell, E. M., Chen, G., Cottone, K., Lapedis, D., & Lee, K. (2007). Impact and the art of motivation maintenance: The effects of contact with beneficiaries on persistence behavior. *Organizational Behavior and Human Decision Pocesses*, 103(1), 53–67. https://doi.org/10.1016/j.obhdp.2006.05.004

Hansen, D. M., Larson, R. W., & Dworkin, J. B. (2003). What adolescents learn in organized youth activities: A survey of self-reported developmental experiences. *Journal of Research on Adolescence*, 13(1), 25–55. https://doi.org/10.1111/1532-7795.1301006

Harmsel-Nieuwenhuis, L. T., Alarslan, G., van Hilvoorde, I., Koelen, M., Super, S., & Verkooijen, K. (2022). Life skills development and transfer amongst socially vulnerable adults through sports: A systematic review. *International Review of Sport and Exercise Psychology*, 1–41. https://doi.org/10.1080/1750984X.2022.2135125

Holt, N., Neely, K., Slater, L., Camiré, M., Côté, J., Fraser-Thomas, J., MacDonald, D., Strachan, L., & Tamminen, K. (2017). A grounded theory of positive youth development through sport based on results from a qualitative meta-study. *International Review of Sport and Exercise Psychology*, 10, 1–49. https://doi.org/10.1080/1750984X.2016.1180704

Lawson, H. A. (2005). Empowering people, facilitating community development, and contributing to sustainable development: The social work of sport, exercise, and physical education programs. *Sport, Education and Society*, 10(1), 135–160. https://doi.org/10.1080/1357332052000308800

Legg, E., & Karner, E. (2021). Development of a model of diversity, equity and inclusion for sport volunteers: An examination of the experiences of diverse volunteers for a national sport governing body. *Sport, Education and Society*, 26(9), 966–981. https://doi.org/10.1080/13573322.2021.1907325

Liden, R. C., & Arad, S. (1996). A power perspective of empowerment and work groups: Implications for human resources management research. *Research in Personnel and Human Resources Management, 14*, 205–251.

Lim, S. Y., & Dixon, M. A. (2017). A conceptual framework of sport participation and women's empowerment. *Managing Sport and Leisure, 22*(5), 400–413. https://doi.org/10.1080/23750472.2018.1499437

Maneka, M. F. (2023). The psychological experience of meaning in life: A systematic scoping review of multi-component conceptualization. *Qualitative Research, 23*(2). https://doi.org/10.1234/qr.v23.i2.16

Maness, M. (2017). A theory of strong ties, weak ties, and activity behavior: Leisure activity variety and frequency. *Transportation Research Record, 2665*(1), 30–39. https://doi.org/10.3141/2665-04

Mor Barak, M. E., Luria, G., & Brimhall, K. C. (2022). What leaders say versus what they do: Inclusive leadership, policy-practice decoupling, and the anomaly of climate for inclusion. *Group & Organization Management, 47*(4), 840–871. https://doi.org/10.1177/10596011211005916

Pierce, S., Gould, D., & Camiré, M. (2016). Definition and model of life skills transfer. *International Review of Sport and Exercise Psychology, 10*(1), 186–211. https://doi.org/10.1080/1750984X.2016.1199727

Ronkainen, N. J., Aggerholm, K., Ryba, T. V., & Allen-Collinson, J. (2020). Learning in sport: From life skills to existential learning. *Sport, Education and Society, 26*(2), 214–227. https://doi.org/10.1080/13573322.2020.1712655

Rosso, B. D., Dekas, K. H., & Wrzesniewski, A. (2010). On the meaningfulness of work: A theoretical integration and review. *Research in Organizational Behavior, 30*, 91–127. https://doi.org/10.1016/j.riob.2010.09.001

Ryan, R. M., & Deci, E. L. (2000). Self-determination theory and the facilitation of intrinsic motivation, social development, and well-being. *American Psychologist, 55*(1), 68–78. https://doi.org/10.1037/0003-066X.55.1.68

Seligman, M. E. P. (2002). Positive psychology, positive prevention, and positive therapy. In C. R. Snyder, & S. J. Lopez (eds.), *Handbook of positive psychology* (pp. 3–9). Oxford University Press.

Shore, L. M., & Chung, B. G. (2022). Inclusive leadership: How leaders sustain or discourage work group inclusion. *Group & Organization Management, 47*(4), 723–754. https://doi.org/10.1177/1059601121999580

Shore, L. M., Randel, A. E., Chung, B. G., Dean, M. A., Holcombe Ehrhart, K., & Singh, G. (2011). Inclusion and diversity in work groups: A review and model for future research. *Journal of Management, 37*(4), 1262–1289. https://doi.org/10.1177/0149206310385943

Spaaij, R., Magee, J., & Jeanes, R. (2014). *Sport and social exclusion in global society*. Routledge.

Spreitzer, G. M. (1995). Psychological empowerment in the workplace: Dimensions, measurement, and validation. *Academy of Management Journal, 38*(5), 1442–1465. https://doi.org/10.2307/256865

Spreitzer, G. M. (2007). Toward the integration of two perspectives: A review of social-structural and psychological empowerment at work. In C. Cooper, & J. Barling (eds.), *The handbook of organizational behavior*. SAGE.

Spreitzer, G. M. (2008). Taking Stock: A review of more than twenty years of research on empowerment at work. In C. Cooper, & J. Barling (eds.), *Handbook of organizational behavior* (pp. 54–73). SAGE.

Spreitzer, G. M., & Doneson, D. (2005). Musings on the past and future of employee empowerment. In T. G. Cummings (ed.), *Handbook of organization development* (pp. 311–324). SAGE.

Stillman, T. F., & Baumeister, R. F. (2009). Uncertainty, belongingness, and four needs for meaning. *Psychological Inquiry*, *20*(4), 249–251. https://doi.org/10.1080/10478400903333544

Stillman, T. F., & Lambert, N. M. (2013). The bidirectional relationship of meaning and belonging. In *The experience of meaning in life: Classical perspectives, emerging themes, and controversies* (pp. 305–315). Springer.

Stone, C. (2018). Utopian community football? Sport, hope and belongingness in the lives of refugees and asylum seekers. *Leisure Studies*, *37*(2), 171–183. https://doi.org/10.1080/02614367.2017.1329336

Tajfel, H., & Turner, J. C. (1986). The social identity theory of intergroup behavior. In S. Worchel & W. G. Austin (eds.), *Psychology of intergroup relations* (pp. 7–24). Nelson-Hall.

Thomas, K. W., & Velthouse, B. A. (1990). Cognitive elements of empowerment: An "interpretive" model of intrinsic task motivation. *Academy of Management Review*, *15*(4), 666–681. https://doi.org/10.2307/258687

Turnnidge, J., Côté, J., & Hancock, D. J. (2014). A socio-ecological approach to understanding life skill development in sport. *International Journal of Sport and Exercise Psychology*, *12*(1), 61–72. https://doi.org/10.1080/1612197X.2014.888786

Van der Veken, K., Lauwerier, E., & Willems, S. (2020). 'To mean something to someone': Sport-for-development as a lever for social inclusion. *International Journal for Equity in Health*, *19*, 1–13. https://doi.org/10.1186/s12939-019-1119-7

Veli Korkmaz, A., van Engen, M. L., Knappert, L., & Schalk, R. (2022). About and beyond leading uniqueness and belongingness: A systematic review of inclusive leadership research. *Human Resource Management Review*, *32*(4), 1–20. https://doi.org/10.1016/j.hrmr.2022.100894

Vertonghen, J., Theeboom, M., Buelens, E., & De Martelaer, K. (2017). Conditions for successfully increasing disadvantaged adolescents' engagement in and development through volunteering in community sport. *Social Inclusion*, *5*(2), 179–197. https://doi.org/10.17645/si.v5i2.895

Whittaker, C. G., & Holland-Smith, D. (2016). Exposing the dark side, an exploration of the influence social capital has upon parental sports volunteers. *Sport, Education and Society*, *21*(3), 356–373. https://doi.org/10.1080/13573322.2014.923832

Wilson, J. (2000). Volunteering. *Annual Review of Sociology*, *26*(1), 215–240. https://doi.org/10.1146/annurev.soc.26.1.215

Wolfgruber, D., Stürmer, L., & Einwiller, S. (2022). Talking inclusion into being: Communication as a facilitator and obstructor of an inclusive work environment. *Personnel Review*, *51*(7), 1841–1860. https://doi.org/10.1108/PR-01-2021-0013

6 The role of leadership for social inclusion policy development in Europe

Introduction

The research question of this study was: *What role does leadership play in promoting social inclusion through sports?* Based on the empirical explorations earlier in this book, working to achieve social inclusion through sport in many ways is a Sisyphean task. Across Europe, policy makers and governments cherish value-based ideals of social inclusion. Unfortunately, these ideals are often out of sync with realities when it comes to funding, priorities, human resources, and collaborative arrangements between sport organizations and stakeholders from other sectors of society. Furthermore, it is difficult to prevent social exclusion by simply including. Leaders in sport organizations in Europe therefore operate under contradictory circumstances. At the same time, we found that the sampled leaders expressed a genuine belief in the idea that sport can make a difference for the good of society, especially if things were a bit different from what they are at present.

More specifically, we found a leadership practice dependent on a stakeholder collective to realize social inclusion projects, while at the same time, leaders would be missed if they disappeared. Whereas leaders are not heroic figures able to solve any challenge, leadership functions must be operated by *someone*. That said, no one-size-fits-all-logic exist. Despite the ambitions of the European Model of Sport (EMS), national and regional variations are vast in terms of resources, funding, organizational characteristics, leadership styles, and the relation between grassroots and elite sport. The connection between societal characteristics and the characteristics of the sport through which inclusion efforts are made must also be considered. Meeting the responsibility as leaders for socially inclusive arenas thus requires from them a broad span of psychological and sociological insights on how social inclusion and exclusion affect groups and individuals in different contexts.

DOI: 10.4324/9781003527848-6

This chapter has been made available under a CC-BY-NC-ND license.

Role of leadership for social inclusion policy development 107

Against this backdrop, the aim of this chapter is to demonstrate how our analysis comes together and can be converted into policy advice on leadership and social inclusion through sport. In Chapter 3, we found that access was about seeing who's not in the room and making efforts to rectify that by considering the relationship between equalizing and differentiating motives. Chapter 4 then discussed how to include those 'sitting at the table' and how they could become 'co-authors' of their own destinies. Thereafter, given that access and participation were in place, Chapter 5 outlined how the lessons from being included could be transferred into experiences relevant to others and the community overall when 'leaving the table.' By combining these findings, the next section discusses how four dimensions of inclusive practices – complexity, collaboration, consideration, and compassion – connect with the three conceptual dimensions of social inclusion as posed by Gidley et al. (2010). Thereafter, we specify implications for policy makers, before the book ends with some limitations of this study and research pointers for the road ahead.

A new look at social inclusion and leadership

Through the stories, examples, and episodes our informants shared with us, we found that social inclusion themes in sport represent a cluster of 'wicked problems' (Rittel & Webber, 1973). These are characterized by competing interpretations of where problems lie, by the uncertainty in causal connections, and, by the new or unforeseen consequences of policy programmes (Sam, 2009). Considering the wider role of sport in social inclusion, where wicked problems, as elsewhere, 'are characterized by disagreement over the very nature of the issues at hand' (Sam, 2009, p. 510), leadership is pivotal due to its bridge-building capacity. Our informants support the notion that, where words are attributed to groups and identities for strategic purposes, combined with labelling, communicating, and addressing social realities and cultural sensitivities, they matter to how we understand the processes, powers, and outcomes involved (Swedberg, 2020). Notably, exclusion is not the opposite of inclusion, as the phenomenon may be a result of voluntarily actions, sanctions, or of knowledge deficiencies on both sides, with the club, on the one hand, being unaware of the needs of those who want to be included and lack of knowledge, on the other, among people on the search for a sporting community about what it has to offer. Regardless of whether the priority is anti-social behaviour or funding issues, grassroots leaders in sport must see the big picture without missing the nuts and bolts of what social inclusion can be for targeted groups. Roberto, from Italy, summarized in many ways our informants' view on leadership and the solution to the question of what type of leadership is needed, by describing it as:

> a set of skills and knowledge that enable you to enable a young person that is interested to be involved in grassroots sport environment, to be leader and so to bring their own ideas, to make them aware of the possibilities also that they can find within grassroots sport and how they can use it in order to meet needs and reach objectives. So in one sense, to give them the tools to make their ideas possible.

Our analysis shows that leaders have a humble view of their own role and express deep trust in the community of organizations and other leaders to work collaboratively towards common goals. A part of this reflective attitude is to acknowledge the limits of leadership. Tasha, from France, said that:

> My leadership is irrelevant to influence social inclusion. Just like anyone else I can contribute by investing time and energy in the [NN] which has a very inclusive social structure with public funding and an affordable membership. But real change can only happen if the whole community gets inclusive: individuals but also clubs, companies...

Meanwhile, Roberto, again:

> You are a leader, you are a manager, maybe, in this case, but you cannot do everything by yourself. So you need to involve all the other departments, for example, of your organization (...) And so the difficulty is to make them understand that there are choices that we need to take that are not just related to the economical or efficiency ways, but are needed because we need to meet those needs.

As a result, our informants view social inclusion dimensions as part of an interlinked whole to which leadership is necessary but where leaders are not irreplaceable. While Chapters 2 and 3, and partly Chapter 4 analyse the sociological circumstances of inclusion as a societal phenomenon, the rest of Chapter 4 and above all, Chapter 5, discuss the psychological mechanisms of participation and empowerment. For leaders, these circumstances and mechanisms represent a substantial challenge for them as translators and shapers of organizational policies and for them being inclusive in their own roles to many diverse groups vulnerable to exclusion. As a result, the three dimensions of social inclusion – access, participation, and empowerment – intersect through commonalities in four ways, called The Four Cs. A summary is presented in Table 6.1.

Table 6.1 European leadership commonalities for social inclusion through sport

	The four Cs	Dimensions of social inclusion		
		Access	Participation	Empowerment
What socially inclusive leaders should concentrate on in relation to	Complexity	Mapping diverse barriers to availability	Seeking representational fairness	Redefining the situation
	Collaboration	Creating a sense of community	Involving stakeholders	Making changes the organizational imperative
	Consideration	Suggesting qualified priorities	Enabling joint forces towards a common cause	Empathizing with those 'on the outside'
	Compassion	Inviting others on their premises	Engaging with prioritized groups	Evoking meaning-making in the grander scheme of things

Elaborating on these Four Cs, the first is an acknowledgement of the *complexity* of having leadership responsibilities for a sport organization. Drawing upon complexity leadership theory, we assumed that these complexities emerge as dilemmas and priorities in respect of the available resources for, and capacities of a community. In addition, the decisions and collaborations necessary to get things done in an organization must be anchored among stakeholders way beyond the organization itself. Hence, with the empirical analysis before us, complexity leadership theory is relevant to a discussion of what type of role sport is going to have in tomorrow's society as inclusion projects concern the three entangled CLT functions of organizations discussed in Chapter 2 – administrative leadership, adaptive leadership, and enabling leadership (Uhl-Bien & Marion, 2009, p. 633). Instead of fighting this complexity and ignoring the interrelation between these functions, this study demonstrates the necessity of integrating them and even more so, the benefits of embracing them as part of a complexity management tool in light of the massive expectations of sport in solving societal issues (see Chapter 1).

The change needed, at least on a leader level, is to utilize this complexity to shape the leadership *purpose* of an organization towards the aims of social inclusion engagements. While leadership in sport is about achieving a desired outcome and creating purpose for the people of the organization and its stakeholders beyond financial gain and quantifiable results (Næss & Svendsen, 2024), CLT owes an intellectual debt to Barth's theory of transactions, as the latter 'bring(s) about what we may regard as the main work of integration in culture because they make actors establish commensurability between the forms of value over which they consummate transactions' (Barth, 2007, p. 8). In Chapter 2, we argued that this type of inclusive engagement among leaders was dependent on the value of transactions (Barth, 1972) between stakeholders in a bigger societal system. As any decision to seek increased value comes with a price, we recall that Barth (1972) argued that we needed 'to commit the simplification of distinguishing between total societies as distinct bodies of people. Rather, we can utilize the relative discontinuities in the networks and premises of interaction to delimit social systems within their larger environment' (Barth, 1972, p. 216). Hence, constraints and incentives for social interaction in sport are entangled with societal forces in a way that 'appears to affect the preferences of individuals at a time prior to that at which the effects of the orientational mechanisms are felt and can coexist with either of the latter mechanisms' (Skvoretz & Conviser, 1974, p. 54). An example was given by Luis, who said that:

> we have stakeholders and organizations who deal with us and who really do it with their best intention but we still see their attitude towards us is that they are doing us a favor, or they are (…) doing charity (…) they are treating it like throwing almost a coin to the poor. And we feel that, okay, of course, we will accept the coin, let's say it like this, because we need to keep our mission, but that's not the objective because, what's more than that, what we believe is that you change and you really support because you see this as an opportunity.

To operationalize this issue, we turn to the second condition, which is to lead by *collaboration*. Although pragmatism seems to be the key tactic for European sport leaders to get things done, it works best when it is combined with directions on where one wants to go. Given the democratic elements of EMS and the national variants, our informants specified that to realize that ideal, sport cannot be confined to its own sector. Community engagement, by contrast, although not always termed that way, was instrumental to most of them. As proposed by Kidd (2008), and further nuanced by Welty Peachey et al. (2019), and as our findings support, for community engagement programmes to lead to social inclusion and be part of solving prominent social issues within an area, it is necessary to involve the targets or beneficiaries of these programmes. According to Coalter (2002), the relation between sport and communities can be related to the growth of sport in communities, by removing barriers, advancing sporting excellence, recruiting local volunteers and so on. Sport and communities can also interact through focus on social outcomes such as general health, reducing crime, building employability and academic skills and so on (Coalter,

2007). Acknowledging the importance of both forms of community engagement, Coalter (2002) underlines the importance of participation and influence sharing when engaging with communities. Specifically, he argues that 'the involvement of local communities in the identification of relevant opportunities can ensure appropriate provision, a sense of ownership, and cooperation – all of which can contribute to the success and sustainability of programmes' (Coalter, 2002, p. 15).

More than twenty years after Coalter wrote this, Anders, one of our Danish informants, said that a requirement for sport, viewed as physical activity and not so much as organized activity coordinated by a set of rules and norms, to be a change factor in society, cross-sectorial alliances are required:

> Our main objective is basically to look beyond the sports sector. Instead of looking inward, we must look outward and bring in people from the education sector, and people from the inclusion sector, and people from the health sector. What can we contribute from a sports perspective to other and broader sectors? So before we talk about inclusion effect, or health effect, or education effect, we are not relevant.

Nevertheless, although Coalter (2002, 2007), centres the importance of participation in sport, the level of participation described rarely extends to consultation. To specify the participatory processes, Coalter (2002) presents examples such as surveys and ensuring representation from the whole local community. More specifically, Corvino et al. (2023) argue that those working with sport and social inclusion should 'consider introducing social workers who act according to the principle of forming alliances between the diverse systems of youth life, namely, the sport system, the family system, and the larger community' (p. 16). According to some of our informants, the local community should not merely be consulted, but should be the drivers of social inclusion programmes. Craig from the UK even goes so far as to say that he considers his organization to be community-led. When asked how he works to develop the different activities in the communities, he explains:

> The first thing is going back to being aware of the communities that we're serving. Have an awareness of demographics, have an awareness of marginalized groups within a society. I'm forever supporting grassroots clubs who want to become more inclusive, but they want to say they are inclusive, but that's just words, but actually in practice, are they on the ground – Including all people from different backgrounds and with ability and needs? So I think as a leader personally what we do is we make sure we listen to our community, and we're almost led by them we're led by the community.

Bernard is also very specific that local programmes need to be led by the local communities themselves. However, he is also specific that the programmes should not only be initiated by the communities. The participants should also play a crucial part in implementing the programmes:

> How do you move away from consultation to actually active participation and co-creation? Just saying, 'hey hence you're gonna participate and I'm gonna listen to you. It's not enough if I listen to you I need you to be part of the process of implementing.

Similarly, Roberto put it well as he claimed that sport and social inclusion were never about sport alone. For him, it was a community thing, where municipalities represented the ideal hub for coordinating social inclusion projects as they:

> can give you an overview where you can also meet and find the other organizations, the other actors of the communities, to involve all of them together with the users in a participatory process. This can be really important because at the end the event, the service, the activity really can meet the needs of all the community.

This could have long-term effects, Roberto argued, while in the opposite case, 'you don't have people that attend so it's not useful and for sure something that won't even last the period of the funding that you bring.' Similarly, Luis from Portugal said that, with reference to physical disabilities, 'I believe this program has much more indirect beneficiaries than direct.' He told the story of a project where a person had first taken part in a leadership programme organized by Luis and his colleagues, and then used the experience to transform the view of disabilities in sport in a country in Eastern Europe:

> Her life changed completely, but majority of people that were impacted are people that we even never will know in our lives, that are the wheelchair user that couldn't go to the match and now they can go to watch their national team.

As such, our leaders underline the importance of making the community participate, as opposed to simply being consulted, if the goal is to increase social inclusion through community engagement programmes.

The third condition is to *consider* the relation between aim, process, and outcome of social inclusion projects without locking in to one or the other. Earlier research on where the weight should be is inconclusive. A study of newcomers to a Canadian winter sport programme found that integration was part of its outcome yet 'not a central feature of the programming'

(Barrick, 2023, p. 720). One result was that participants raised concerns about the integrative potential of 'winter sport participation more generally instead of specific programme examples' (Barrick, 2023, p. 720). Most of our informants, however, did not distinguish between goal, process, or outcome of social inclusion in their daily work. Yet, as exemplified in Chapters 3–5, this could be a tactical move from leaders to get funded or, by arguing in favour of a broadened concept of 'access,' to secure meaningful participation underpinning the aim to empower people beyond programmatic interventions in people's lives. Distinctions between the components of inclusion were more functional than substantial to the notion of what social inclusion is. Aila from Finland made some interesting reflections in that respect: 'Do you ever come to the finish line? It's a process. A journey. You have to do it. But you never come to the destination.' Stephen from the UK, preferred to see it as an outcome: 'Knowing why you design your programmes and what change you want to see is key to potentially creating impact.' Others said that planning was key. For Lydia from Greece, an important leadership task is to:

> be very, very careful and very, very precise on our goals. And it depends on the leader and what the goal is that he or she wants to achieve. Usually it's a he, which is another big issue because leaders are male. Leadership is a masculine word. at least in my world. So I think it depends on what they want.

Similarly, Roberto says that: 'The ideal project works so well that the people that attend it know how to repeat, to reply and of course to bring it throughout the years because it's something that belongs to the community.' Finally, being clear about your ambitions is not merely statement-driven; it can also avoid misunderstandings. In Slovenia, our informant, Jon tells us, judo clubs have for more than two decades offered programmes directed towards, for example, children with autism or people with cerebral palsy. The major benefit of these programmes, according to Jon, is that nobody 'ever leaves a community in which they feel good, are accepted and respected, and are enabled to contribute, advance, and grow.' The secret to making this work, Jon states, is that 'the people we include in judo practice are full members of the club with equal rights and duties. We consistently avoid any unnecessary labeling of judokas and any type of discrimination.' While it might be less inclusive in a functional sense by being open to all, it is in return wholly transparent about the premises for taking part. In other words, the takeaway from this element is to say what you mean and mean what you say as a leader working with social inclusion through sport.

The fourth is (organizational) *compassion*. For leadership on a meso-level analysis, this view is relatable to a common challenge in inclusion research: to make individuals, groups, and even organizations feel unique and a sense of belonging at the same time. This element is complementary to the other three Cs because, as noted by Davey and Gordon (2017), 'by focusing only on the fact-of-the-matter participation' as a proxy for inclusion, we 'cannot capture the subtle, implicit aspect of exclusion' (p. 5). A central tenet of the relationship between social inclusion and empowerment in an organizational compassion context is that empowered individuals are more likely to set goals, find pathways, and be motivated to follow these routes (Egan et al., 2008). To reduce dropout, Back et al. (2022) underline the importance of 'a high-quality motivational climate facilitating, for example, the basic psychological needs' (p. 9). Linking this back to Chapter 5 in particular, our data support Lambert et al.'s (2013) finding that it was the subjective feeling of belonging, and not the exposure to social relationships per se, that was decisive for the individual's perception of meaningfulness. Larger correlational studies also confirm this relationship (Moynihan et al., 2023) while qualitative studies have found that 'a sense of belonging occurred through deepened group sharing in a safe social environment, understanding, acceptance and support. In addition, expanding one's social network and healing through laughter and fun were meaningful aspects of the group' (Lund et al., 2019, p. 63). Moreover, they found that meaning making 'occurred through group participation as participants experienced positive personal contrasts. This especially related to feeling less alone, more connected, supported, respected, and worthy' (Lund et al., 2019, p. 64).

Seemingly, a means to do so is an organizational surrounding characterized by a view of compassion that is 'more than the sum of aggregated individual workers' compassionate behavior (…) and involves an ongoing, systemic capacity to notice, feel, and respond to suffering' (McAllum et al., 2023). Drawing on conservation of resources theory (Hobfoll, 1989), Simpson et al. (2024) argue that the aim of organizational compassion as leadership motive is to reduce causes of 'suffering,' that is, people's loss of personal and social resources needed to achieve goals. To that end, our informants demonstrate the practical implications of the NEAR framework – without anyone naming it as such – which involves noticing, empathising, appraising, and responding (Simpson et al., 2024, p. 8). In a social inclusion context, this prevents people's need for being part of a collective running contrary to their perception of their own selves. Lydia underlined for people in her workshops that being a refugee is not an identity:

> I don't talk with Greek students about refugees. This is exactly what I say. This is not their identity. It's just the status that I want to be temporary. It's a status that we are potentially all in danger of having. Ukrainians did not believe five years ago that they would become

refugees. But being an athlete is an identity because many people self-define their personality by their ability in sports.

In the bigger scheme of things, this element reveals how the core motivation for leaders practicing organizational compassion is to generate meaningfulness among those involved. A final example came from Judit from Slovenia:

> Many times I see that, especially people with intellectual disability, they're like suns, like sunshine, like, you know, they don't know how to make tactics, you know, even in judo, they don't have any tactic. They just do what they learned. And even in life, they don't measure, they don't try to fake or something. They just are who they are. And with that, we are getting from them so much more than they are getting from us.

Policy implications and priorities

Understanding policy as 'an action program intended to reify a priority structure' (Meehan, 1985, p. 307), two types of findings from this study shed light on future needs. On a *programmatic level*, it supports the criticisms against the EMS that it is not adapted to the diversity of sport organizations in Europe (see Chapter 1). Analysing the status of the model on the assumption that it is suitable for increasing physical activity, a report by Rask et al. (2024) warns about becoming too dependent on it 'as the core framework for policy development' because then it 'runs the risk of establishing a blind spot that does not cater for the large share of European citizens outside this structure' (p. 23), such as fitness centres or outdoor activities. What is more, there are major differences within the EU member states when it comes to the settings for sport and exercise. Nordic countries have much higher participation rates than Southern European countries, while the proportion of sports club memberships are much higher in Western European countries than in Eastern Europe, as people there often exercise at home or while commuting. Hence, the authors postulate that 'differences in the overall participation levels between countries to some degree can be related to how equal citizens' participation in sport and exercise is across gender and age groups' (Rask et al., 2024, p. 23).

At the same time, a Europe-wide push for social inclusion through sport is highly desired by our informants, if it is adapted to national needs. One reason is that it might have an equalizing effect. Whereas some governments, as in the UK for example, have been actively promoting sport as a means to social inclusion and community development through funding schemes and educational reforms (Crisp, 2020), other countries have a trickle-down model where inclusion projects in grassroots sport depend on elite sport performances. Many of our informants, moreover, underlined national differences and international trends. For example, Nina, thought the Eastern European mindset influenced the view of sport as hard-boiled competitive arena negatively, by stigmatizing those who leave sport because of that competitiveness as what she referred to as 'snowflakes.' These potentially equalizing policy dimensions are hard to grasp within the current EMS, as it fails to consider the diversity of social inclusion efforts. Our informant Anders said that:

> we think this is a problem. It [EMS] becomes an organizational monopoly structure, and a financial straitjacket by only looking at the connection between the elite and the rest. In reality, the best investment you can make is to get people to participate. So, it is a political issue for us. We never talk about the European Sport Model as the basis for inclusion. In fact, I think it can prevent it. Because it is based on an understanding of competition and sports, which is about other things than citizens with special needs, or with special prerequisites.

This comment points back to what we discussed in Chapter 2, where statistics about physical activity in Europe told a story about inclusion and exclusion that questions the structural limitations of organized sport. Although sport organizations serve important integrative functions in society, they are not always ideally designed to manage the diversity of physical activity preferences. Consequently, there is no agreement on 'how far the features of the European Sport Model can help to preserve sport as a public good and realise policy goals through sport' (Sennett et al., 2022, p. 9), as the question should be asked differently. Instead, as argued by several of our informants, social inclusion has a more natural place in an organizational structure resembling Scheerder's (2020) church model which consists of four levels: grassroots sport, compulsory sport, mass sport, and, at the apex, professional sport. However, due to the mixing of levels and priorities in EMS as well as the wicked problems involved, there is no clear agreement among our informants or among policy makers across Europe on which problem related to social inclusion and grassroots sports is most acute, why it has emerged, or what it would take to solve it.

This brings us to the second policy implication, which is about *leadership priorities*. While the church model is visually appealing, it says less about how levels intersect, for example, in terms of the relation between grassroots funding, membership figures of federations, and elite performance. If social inclusion continues to be a part of sport's responsibility and capacity, these issues must be dealt with inductively before designing new European models in terms of agreeing on where to restart. In that connection, we propose a priority structure based on what our informants said about solving the challenges ahead to exploit the benefits of a continent-wide push for social inclusion, which could serve as the basis for remodelling the EMS. The first priority is relevant grassroots involvement. Lamenting the lack of funding for grassroots sport in Europe, Anders said it like this:

> We have the crisis of trumping our case, and I think that will be our biggest challenge. We don't know what's coming, but something will probably come. And then it is difficult to be in the sports sector, I think. So (…) instead of speaking the political case and helping when there is a crisis…we have to protect the funding for the sports sector because it is disappearing. So relevance will probably be our biggest challenge going forward.

In line with Crisp's argument (2020) that 'promotion of key outcomes related to empowerment match well with the aims of community sport projects, in particular the manner in which it can demonstrate positive developmental changes in individuals, stronger civic links, and an improved quality of community life' (p. 224), we argue that social inclusion through sport cannot be a one-ship mission. Instead, metaphorically speaking, the entire fleet must be coordinated and put into movement if social inclusion is to happen and determine whether sport will remain as the relevant arena for it.

The second priority is to strategically mix targeted and general inclusion tools. Despite the risk of re-stigmatization, our findings suggest that it is better to target groups and merge them into mainstream activities than trying a one-size-fits-all approach or not aiming for inclusion at all assuming it will take care of itself due to team sport's inclusive characteristics. Kunz et al. (2021) write that:

> The crucial moment in these initiatives is actually transferring participants from exclusive groups into regular services, which is of course easier when the latter are open to diversity. Therefore, exclusive support and inclusive programs are not to be seen as alternative but as complementary.
>
> (Kunz et al., 2021, p. 18)

In practice, as exemplified by Luis who facilitated two leadership programmes – one for people with disabilities and another open to all – these two elements can be planned to merge down the road. But this requires a clear mission. On the one hand, he said:

> To include the disability community inside the sports industry, we believe that that we should keep it just for disabled people (...) because in the end what we want is to include a specific group inside an industry with that problem. If we open it for non-disabled people, then we will be reducing our objective because we'll be having less disabled people (...) across the sports world.

On the other hand, talking about the other programme, he said:

> It's open to everyone, because here we believe it's our mission to create an environment where (...) even if there are differences (...) we all have the same access. You have this objective, and these are the means that will get you there. Although they differ, they sort of seek the same outcome.

To avoid working along parallel lines, better coordination is needed. One example is the confusing information about the sources of funding available to organizations, as well as about their opportunities for cooperation with other external actors both nationally and within Europe (Future ++, 2020, p. 43). A Swedish informant, Sebastian, therefore called for more systematic approaches to the topic, as this was the only way of realizing the ambitions imposed upon them by their funders and policy developers:

> I think that sport [organizations], at least in Sweden, is built on the idea that you want to contribute to society. They want to offer lifespan development based on a health perspective, a social perspective and more. And with that, it goes in line that inclusion is an important part of maintaining and legitimizing the whole image and the whole idea of sport. So not working with these parts is not a choice. You have to do it. But to be able to do that, I, and many of the colleagues I work with, believe that it is important to do it systematically.

Obvious as it might seem, this is a task which requires expertise and networks, which leads us to the third priority: make leaders great again. Sport leadership is a rarity in studies and policy documents about social inclusion through sport. But as translators, mediators, and 'chairpersons' of the meso crossroads between group processes and contextual factors (see Chapter 2), they occupy roles that require a finely tuned management of emotion-based and task-based responsibilities. Although one biographical analysis of global sport leaders paints a gloomy picture of their ethical and democratic qualities (Bayle & Clastres, 2018), other studies find that sport leaders can epitomize the claim that there is no better source of meaning at work than having a heart for its mission. Keeping this heart warm, as it were, is according to our informants not dependent on leadership style, strategies or credentials; it is about *caring for* people.

(Næss & Svendsen, 2024, p. 157)

In that context, we believe that our informants had some relevant experiences for the road ahead. Luis said that, from a disability perspective, leaders should try questioning themselves:

What we do already, is it that we can do something better? Because you are already seeing disability as part of your mission, of your scope, my suggestion here is that he or she of course asks him or herself what they do already for disability and is there anything that they can do more.

Similarly, Roberto said that:

We have few resources for staffing, so everyone must be a jack of all trades. You can be the manager, you can be the trainer, you can be the social worker, but at the moment you always have to look in the eyes of those who are in your project at any level.

Beginning with the perception and a mission to convince others to put a given topic 'within the circle,' as he put it, was discussed in Chapters 3–5 as the opportunity to set the agenda for those waiting to be included. Leaders are, first, instrumental in working for the creation of access by marginalized groups to where decisions are made. Second, they are key to translating access into participation by inviting representatives to not only sit at the table, but also advocate solutions which make them part in the operationalization of decisions. Last, in terms of empowerment, they are central to following up on whether this combination of access and participation can create indirect benefits and personal development, both as documentation of the initiated projects and as learning material for future projects.

Limitations of this study and avenues for further research

Reaching the end of this book, we can document a European-wide belief in sport as a catalyst for social progress and well-being. This belief, moreover, creates results that are not always tangible or measurable, but which would, had they been absent, have made a gaping hole in the lives of those involved. For sure, arguing that social inclusion through sport can be improved by research 'may be implicated in perpetuating the notion that sport can be used as some sort of magic pill which can cure a variety of social issues' (Misener et al., 2022, p. 323). There is, however, no conflict between adhering to the highest standards of research ethics and having an ambition to have an impact on society by suggesting remedies for things that don't work and emphasizing the things that do. By advocating a critical, yet hopeful approach to what social inclusion through sport can bring about in terms of social change, this book has contributed to studies of sport and social change by bridging the called-for theory-practice divide among sport management scholars (Love et al., 2021). At the same time, the study has identified some of the antecedents of limits to inclusion which are also avenues for further research.

First, complete inclusion will never take place. Although much can be solved, there will always be exclusionary processes, as inclusion requires some criteria for being included in the first place (Hansen, 2012). Sport is, in this case, paradoxical with its rules for participation, not least connected to gender, age, and physical ability. Yet, some form of eligibility criteria – such as the division of football players into teams – are necessary to create a 'We.' But where to draw the line? Second, having the power to define the ones to be included and what they are to be included in produces a danger of assimilation into the majority culture. Sometimes, this might be intentional, a means of cohesion, whereas, in other cases, it might be unintentional, as when individualizing the responsibility for successful inclusion (Simpson & Price, 2010). Meanwhile, leaving the responsibility to the state can also lead to disempowering people since it fails to recognize their contribution to society. Third, targeting groups in need of inclusion might end up by stigmatizing them or reinforcing stereotypes. For example, 'immigrants' is not a homogenous group of people, not even within ethnic or religious groups, or families (Bilali, 2014). Fourth, inclusion projects can contain elements of tokenism, defined as 'a pattern of activity meant to foster the illusion of inclusivity within social systems where a dominant group is pressured to share resources (e.g., privilege, power, commodities) with a historically excluded group' (Drenten et al., 2023, p. 3). As an example, tokenized individuals may fall victim to 'role entrapment' which, in the case of social inclusion projects, results in people being 'that guy' who is there to secure an image of representative participation on behalf of a marginalized group.

Yet, these challenges are not insurmountable, either as research topics or practical tasks. Rather, they constitute a grid of researchable areas that it is necessary to explore if leaders of social inclusion, either as bearers of a top-down idea by the European Commission or as entrepreneurs of a minor project in a rural community, are to serve its promise and purpose. What is more, if one supports the idea of inclusion as a morally sound idea which might also be beneficial for a socially cohesive society, this book demonstrates that there is no reason to let go of inclusion aims through sport.

In a Europe currently characterized by increasing threats to social equality, democracy, and rule of law (Civil Liberties Union for Europe, 2024; Eick et al., 2024), using sport as an incubator of the opposite – regardless of the reach of its idealistic connotations – is too good an opportunity to waste. To that end, as voiced by Sabine when asked about any problematic aspects of inclusion: 'I think there's no other way. I thought of it the opposite way. And I thought, well, if not inclusion, then what?'

References

Back, J., Johnson, U., Svedberg, P., McCall, A., & Ivarsson, A. (2022). Drop-out from team sport among adolescents: A systematic review and meta-analysis of prospective studies. *Psychology of Sport and Exercise*, *61*, 1–11. https://doi.org/10.1016/j.psychsport.2022.102205

Barrick, S. (2023). 'It's just about having fun'? Interrogating the lived experiences of newcomers To Canada in introductory winter sport programmes. *International Review for the Sociology of Sport*, *58*(4), 703–724. https://doi.org/10.1177/10126902231156143

Barth, F. (1972). Analytical dimensions in the comparison of social organizations. *American Anthropologist*, *74*(1/2), 207–220. https://doi.org/10.1525/aa.1972.74.1-2.02a01720

Barth, F. (2007). Overview: Sixty years in anthropology. *Annual Review of Anthropology*, *36*, 1–16. https://doi.org/10.1146/annurev.anthro.36.081406.094407

Bayle, E., & Clastres, P. (eds.). (2018). *Global sport leaders: A biographical analysis of international sport management*. Springer.

Bilali, R. (2014). The downsides of national identification for minority groups in intergroup conflicts in assimilationist societies. *The British Journal of Social Psychology*, *53*(1), 21–38. https://doi.org/10.1111/bjso.12012

Civil Liberties Union for Europe (2024). *Liberties Rule of Law Report 2024*. https://dq4n3btxmr8c9.cloudfront.net/files/oj7hht/Liberties_Rule_Of_Law_Report_2024_FULL.pdf

Coalter, F. (2002). *Sport and community development: A manual*. Research Report no. 86. Sport Scotland. https://www.sportni.net/wp-content/uploads/2013/03/Sport_and_community_Development_A_manual.pdf

Coalter, F. (2007). *A wider social role for sport: Who's keeping the score?* Routledge.

Corvino, C., D'Angelo, C., & Gozzoli, C. (2023). Social work and social inclusion in sports-based programs: A qualitative study. *Journal of Social Work*, *23*(6), 1099–1117. https://doi.org/10.1177/14680173231197933

Crisp, P. (2020). Autonomy, pro-social behaviour, and working to the future: How coaches in the community can model 'next' practice for their participants. *Managing Sport and Leisure*, *26*(5), 362–376. https://doi.org/10.1080/23750472.2020.1829988

Davey, S. & Gordon, S. (2017). Definitions of social inclusion and social exclusion: The invisibility of mental illness and the social conditions of participation. *International Journal of Culture and Mental Health*, *10*(3), 229–237. https://doi.org/10.1080/17542863.2017.1295091

Drenten, J., Harrison, R. L., & Pendarvis, N. J. (2023). More gamer, less girl: Gendered boundaries, tokenism, and the cultural persistence of masculine dominance. *Journal of Consumer Research*, *50*(1), 2–24, https://doi.org/10.1093/jcr/ucac046

Egan, L. A., Butcher, J., & Ralph, K. (2008). Hope as a basis for understanding the benefits and possibilities of community engagement. In *Australian Universities Community Engagement Alliance National Conference 2008: Engaging for a sustainable future* (pp. 33–40). Australian Universities Community Engagement Alliance Inc.

Eick, G. M., Im, Z. J., & Leschke, J. (2024). Towards social Europe? Obstacles and opportunities in the multi-level governance of welfare states. *Social Policy & Administration*, *58*(4), 545–553. https://doi.org/10.1111/spol.13046

Future ++ (2020). *Future ++ handbook. Sport and social inclusion: Future for children++*. https://future2plus.eu/wp-content/uploads/2023/12/FUTURE-HANDBOOK-ENGLISH-VERSION.pdf

Gidley, J., Hampson, G., Wheeler, L., & Bereded-Samuel, E. (2010). Social inclusion: Context, theory and practice. *The Australasian Journal of University-Community Engagement*, *5*(1), 6–36.

Hansen, J. H. (2012). Limits to inclusion. *International Journal of Inclusive Education*, *16*(1), 89–98. https://doi.org/10.1080/13603111003671632

Hobfoll, S. E. (1989). Conservation of resources: A new attempt at conceptualizing stress. *American Psychologist*, *44*(3), 513–524. https://doi.org/10.1037/0003-066X.44.3.513

Kidd, B. (2008). A new social movement: Sport for development and peace. *Sport in Society*, *11*(4), 370–380. https://doi.org/10.1080/17430430802019268

Kunz, A., Meier, I., Nicoletti, I., Philipp, S., & Star, K. (2021). *The toolkit for equality. City policies against racism*. ETC Graz. https://www.eccar.info/sites/default/files/document/12_Toolkit-en-Sports.pdf

Lambert, N. M., Stillman, T. F., Hicks, J. A., Kamble, S., Baumeister, R. F., & Fincham, F. D. (2013). To belong is to matter: Sense of belonging enhances meaning in life. *Personality and Social Psychology Bulletin*, *39*(11), 1418–1427. https://doi.org/10.1177/0146167213499186

Love, A., Bernstein, S. B., & King-White, R. (2021). 'Two heads are better than one': A continuum of social change in sport management. *Sport Management Review*, *24*(2), 345–364. https://doi.org/10.1016/j.smr.2020.02.005

Lund, K., Hultqvist, J., Bejerholm, U., Argentzell, E., & Eklund, M. (2019). Group leader and participant perceptions of balancing everyday life, a group-based lifestyle intervention for mental health service users. *Scandinavian Journal of Occupational Therapy*, *27*(6), 462–473. https://doi.org/10.1080/11038128.2018.1551419

McAllum, K., Fox, S., Ford, J. L., & Roeder, A. C. (2023). Communicating compassion in organizations: A conceptual review. *Frontiers in Communication*, *8*, 1144045. https://doi.org/10.3389/fcomm.2023.1144045

Meehan, E. J. (1985). Policy: Constructing a definition. *Policy Sciences*, *18*(4), 291–311. https://doi.org/10.1007/BF00135916

Misener, L., Rich, K., & Pearson, E. (2022). Tensions and opportunities in researching social change in sport management. *Sport Management Review*, *25*(2), 323–340. https://doi.org/10.1080/14413523.2021.1902123

Moynihan, A., Guinote, A., & Igou, E. R. (2023). Relational dynamics and meaning in life: Dominance predicts perceived social support, belongingness, and meaning in life. *Personality and Individual Differences*, *211*. https://doi.org/10.1016/j.paid.2023.112249

Næss, H. E., & Svendsen, M. (2024). 'We are not selling soap here, you know': Eight humanistic leadership qualities in sport. *Leadership*, *20*(3), 144–161. https://doi.org/10.1177/17427150241237925

Rask, S., Le Coq, C., & Storm, R. K. (2024). *European sport: One or several sporting realities?* Play the Game. https://www.playthegame.org/media/0nwbrzf3/european-sport.pdf

Rittel, H. W. J., & Webber, M. M. (1973). Dilemmas in a general theory of planning. *Policy Sciences*, *4*, 155–169. https://doi.org/10.1007/BF01405730

Sam, M. P. (2009). The public management of sport. *Public Management Review*, *11*(4), 499–514. https://doi.org/10.1080/14719030902989565

Scheerder, J. (2020). Conclusion: Established models of European sport revisited from a socio-politological approach. In N. R. Porro, S. Martelli, & A. Testa (eds.), *Sport, welfare and social policy in the European Union*. Routledge.

Sennett, J., Le Gall, A., Kelly, G., Cottrill, R., Goffredo, S., & Spyridopoulous, K. (2022). *Study on the European Sport model. A report to the European Commission.* https://www.sportesalute.eu/images/studie-dati-dello-sport/schede/2022/90-study-europeansportmodel.pdf

Simpson, A. V., Cunha, M. P., Clegg, S., Rego, A., & Berti, M. (2024). *Organizational compassion: A relational perspective*. Routledge.

Simpson, G., & Price, V. (2010). From inclusion to exclusion: Some unintended consequences of valuing people. *British Journal of Learning Disabilities*, *38*(3), 180–186. https://doi.org/10.1111/j.1468-3156.2009.00572.x

Skvoretz, J. V., & Conviser, R. H. (1974). Interests and alliances: A reformulation of Barth's models of social organization. *Man*, *9*(1), 53–67. https://doi.org/10.2307/2800036

Swedberg, R. (2020). On the use of definitions in sociology. *European Journal of Social Theory*, *23*(3), 431–445. https://doi.org/10.1177/1368431019831855

Uhl-Bien, M., & Marion, R. (2009). Complexity leadership in bureaucratic forms of organizing: A meso model. *The Leadership Quarterly*, *20*, 631–650. https://doi.org/10.1016/j.leaqua.2009.04.007

Welty Peachey, J., Schulenkorf, N., & Spaaij, R. (2019). Sport for social change: Bridging the theory–practice divide. *Journal of Sport Management*, *33*(5), 361–365. https://doi.org/10.1123/jsm.2019-0291

Index

Pages in **bold** refer to tables.

abductive 16, 26
adaptive leadership 24, 41, 109
administrative leadership 24, 41, 109
assimilation 7, 10, 47–48, 84, 99, 120
autonomy 4, 23, 47, 94–98, **100**

Bandura 66, 69–70, 79
barriers 21, 29, 34, 36–40, 42, 46, 57, 63, 66, 92, 109–110
Barth, Fredrik 18–20, 25, 48, 110
belongingness 25
boundary condition 63–65

capability approach 9
community engagement 55, 110–112
compassion 107, 109, 113–115
competitiveness 38, 85–86, 116
complex adaptive systems (CAS) 24
complexity leadership theory (CLT) 17, 49, 109
constructive controversy 41, 48, 51
corporate social responsibility (CSR) 5
Council of the European Union 3, 7, 43

decision-making 8, 40–41, 43, 48–49, 51
differentiating 45, 50, 107
disability 21, 35, 40, 42–43, 59, 82–83, 94, 97, 115, 118–119

enabling leadership 24, 26, 41
Eurobarometer 22
European Commission 2–3, 26, 37
European Model of Sport 1, 20, 22, 34, 85, 106
European Union 3, 7, 11, 43

immigrants 2, 66, 81, 87, 96, 120
inclusive leadership 17, 24–25, 42–43, 61, 64, 70, 94
influence sharing 61, 63–64, 72, 111
institutional logics 20

key informant 26

LGBTQ+ 46, 80
life skills 66, 87–90, **100**
loyalty 67–68

marginalized 2, 25, 45, 58–60, 65, 69–70, 72, 76–77, 82, 92, 97, 111, 119–120
meaningfulness 35, 72, 77–79, 83, 99, **100**, 114–115
mentoring 69–70, 90
minority 22, 49, 51, 58, 60

neoliberal 25

opportunity 9–10, 17, 39, 55, 70, 93–95, 98, 110, 119, 121

parents 21, 58, 65–66, 82–84, 91–92, 97–98
participative leadership 67–68
phenomenological inquiry 26
policymakers 44
positive discrimination 25, 45–47
priority structure 115, 117
pseudo participation 61–62
psychological empowerment 77–79, 83, 99
psychological safety 67–68, **71**
purpose 19, 24, 79, 91, 109

refugees 60, 76, 80–81, 85, 87–88, 90, 92–93, 95, 114–115
representation 41–42, 45, 56, 62, 70, 111
role modeling 86

self-efficacy 6, 9, 50, 64, 66, 68–72, 79, 87
social cognitive theory 70
social cohesion 4, 10, 36, 39, 80, 89
social complexity 10, 16, 19
social identities 7, 84, **100**
social identity 47, 84, 99

social justice theory 56, 59–60
socio-economic 38, 40, 49–50, 90, **100**
Sport-for-all 4
sport for development 5, 10, 57, 91
Spreitzer 77–79, 87, 90–91, 94
stakeholders 3, 5–6, 20, 22, 25, 28–29, 35, 39, 43, 50, **71**, 87, 106, 109–110

transactions 17, 19–20, 40, 110

uniqueness 25, 47, 86
United Nations Department of Economic and Social Affairs (UNDESA) 21, 43

vicarious experiences 69
voice 56, 64, 66, 69, **71**
volunteering 4, 38, 42, 62, 65–66, 91–92, 94, **100**
vulnerable 2, 6, 10, 55, 57, 60, 82, 87, 99, **100**, 108

wicked problems 107, 116

Printed in the United States
by Baker & Taylor Publisher Services